The
Bread Machine
Bakery Book

ALSO BY RICHARD W. LANGER

The After-Dinner Gardening Book
Grow It!
Grow It Indoors
The Joy of Camping

The
Bread Machine
Bakery Book

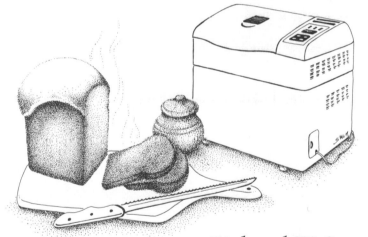

Richard W. Langer

Illustrations by Susan McNeill

LITTLE, BROWN AND COMPANY ❖ BOSTON ❖ TORONTO ❖ LONDON

First Edition

Library of Congress Cataloging-in-Publication Data

Langer, Richard W.
    The bread machine bakery book / Richard W. Langer. — 1st ed.
        p.   cm.
    Includes index.
    ISBN 0-316-51388-1
    1. Bread.
    TX769.L27   1991
    641.8'15 — dc20   91-25904

10   9

MV-NY

Designed by Jeanne Abboud

*Published simultaneously in Canada by Little, Brown
& Company (Canada) Limited*

PRINTED IN THE UNITED STATES OF AMERICA

To the whole family —
Susan, Genevieve, Tanya, Revell, and the dogs,
Crisscross and Zechy —
who spent months on a bread diet

Contents

The
Bread Machine
Bakery Book

1 · Hey, I Bake Real Bread; Why Would I Use One of Those Machines?

FOR YEARS I'VE ENJOYED the pleasure of baking bread in our country kitchen, kneading and fussing with the dough while watching the horses outside mowing down the lawn that I never get around to mowing myself. So one would think I'd be one of the last people in the world to use a bread machine. But I do. They make sense, I've found, for even ardent bakers.

Bread making is not a daily activity for most people, and never has been. In eastern Finland, for instance, from ancient times to the present, the tasty, dark *hapanleipä* with its distinctive hole in the center has traditionally been baked but twice a year. Hundreds of the flat loaves would be suspended from a pole threaded through the holes and stored in the granary or larder. Needless to say, by the time another baking marathon was due, the bread had acquired some hardiness — and so had the Finnish teeth, renowned for their pearly whiteness and durability.

In the Currier and Ives New England of the era before the turn of the century, bread was baked once or twice a week. At least that was the norm for most rural families. Urban families had given up baking, electing to buy fresh loaves as needed from the baker.

Then came preservatives and supermarkets. Bread gave way to baked foam only a little less enduring and flavorful than plastic.

So, nostalgic for that special treat unmatched by newer sub-stitutes — a loaf of bread fresh and fragrant from the oven — people began baking again. But baking done every day can turn from a pleasant task to tedium. Besides, it's only on weekends that most of us have the hours required to enjoy guiding the yeast through its stages of leavening, and by Wednesday or Thursday, staleness has overcome the result of our efforts. Let's face it, in an era in which *Time* magazine has made stress a cover story, finding enough hours on a daily basis to bake bread is not something the average individual can indulge in even thinking about. Enter the bread machines.

I still bake braids and rings the traditional way most Saturdays, because there are many things that a bread machine cannot do. It's not a substitute for home baking. But it's a great addition to it. On weekday evenings I often fill the machine before going to bed, set the timer so the bread will be finished just as we're getting up, and for breakfast we have a fresh, hot loaf.

Much to the chagrin of my wife, Susan, I then proceed to make toast of this wonderful loaf. I can see her point of view, but fresh bread like this makes *real* toast. Most people have never tasted *real* toast, crisp and desert-dry on the outside, moist and soft on the inside. It beckons the taste buds to smile, even when the day is gray and dreary outside.

Apart from toast for breakfast, the freshly baked loaves in all their possible variety can turn a simple meal of soup and bread into a quick, economical repast of epicurean proportions. And coming home from work to the aroma of fresh herb bread may not be exactly like coming home from school when one was nine or ten or thereabouts to Mom's freshly baked cookies set out with a glass of milk, but it's spirit-warmingly close. It's also surely far more homey and comforting for today's latchkey children, who must let them-selves in after school because both parents are away at work, to return to a kitchen redolent of cinnamon or chocolate from a loaf of raisin pumpernickel or two-chocolates bread cheerfully doing its thing in a bread machine than to return to a cold empty house.

Come to think of it, I wouldn't be surprised to see the more enterprising of real estate agents soon buying up bread machines so they could arrange to have the aroma of baking bread wafting from the kitchens of houses they are showing. Our sense of smell is one of our most primal faculties, awakening all kinds of nostalgic memories and emotions. We are really quite vulnerable to scents.

On a less subjective plane, a bread machine makes a great deal of practical economic sense. The ingredients for even the richest loaf of homemade bread cost but a fraction of what the store-bought finished product brings. So within a year the machine should have paid for itself. Meanwhile there will have been a steady supply of nutritious, flavorsome bread from its obliging, compact oven — all as free as it can be of additives and questionable ingredients. With a bread machine, you know what's cooking. And you can key its output to your mood and inclination.

2 · On Flour and Other Ingredients

THERE'S FLOUR, and then there's bread flour. The big difference between the two consists of the amount of gluten, a protein that becomes elastic and sticky with the addition of moisture, present in the flour. Gluten is necessary for most breads; the special high-gluten flour known as bread flour, touted by bread machine manufacturers, is not. I have used regular unbleached flour and bread flour interchangeably in almost all the recipes that follow. The one place where I do suggest using bread flour is in a recipe with a high proportion of oatmeal, which seems to benefit from a dose of the higher-gluten flour.

By all means use bread flour if that's what you have around. For that matter, you can use bleached flour instead of the unbleached, if you prefer. I just like the latter because the bleaching process involves chlorinating the flour; unbleached flour is whitened naturally, through aging.

Speaking of aging, whole-wheat and rye flours, unlike white or all-purpose flour, because they include the germ of the grain, contain perishable oils that, if allowed to go rancid, can add a bitter taste to your bread. These flours really need refrigeration if they are to be kept around for more than a month or so, or even less long during hot summers.

However, for best results, the ingredients for a loaf of bread should be at room temperature before they are used anyway, so if the flour is in the refrigerator along with the yeast, eggs, milk, and maybe butter, you need only remember to take it out when you take those out.

Flour can also be kept in the freezer for long-term storage. Here you will have to remember to remove it a little earlier, but that's presumably not an insurmountable obstacle. One thing that's helpful is to freeze the flour in small, more or less recipe-sized bags rather than in large containers.

Whole-wheat flour incorporates the entire wheat kernel, including the vital bran with its fiber. The light brown color of this flour derives from the bran and the germ. Breads using whole wheat do not rise as rapidly and as far as white-flour dough.

Rye flour produces bread with a fine texture and a chewy crust. The higher the proportion of rye flour in a recipe, the smaller the loaf will be, because rye has a low gluten content. However, it's a rich, dark, flavorful flour that adds a lot of zest to bread.

Rye comes in a number of grades, the two most common ones being medium and the darker pumpernickel. Pumpernickel is the coarser of the two and contains a lot of bran. It's a nice flour for dense breads. Unfortunately, it's not readily available in this country. So for all the recipes in this volume calling for rye flour, including the pumpernickel recipes, I've used the medium variety, usually labeled simply as rye and available at most supermarkets. Some health-food stores do carry real pumpernickel flour, and it can be substituted for the medium rye in the recipes with good results.

Rye flour is measured unsifted in old-time recipes. I've extended that handy timesaving axiom to the other flours as well. In the recipes in this volume, a cupful of flour means a cupful of flour as it comes shaken or spooned from the bag.

Cornmeal is another bread ingredient readily available at the supermarket. It is actually a flour, but is commonly referred to as a meal because of its gritty texture.

The color of cornmeal is traditionally divided by the Mason-Dixon line. North of that boundary, the meal is yellow; south of it, white. For baking purposes the two are interchangeable — but don't try to tell that to anyone with set ideas about the rightful color of the meal.

Whole-grain cornmeal, stone- or water-ground, contains the

germ, and so profits from storage in the refrigerator. Degermed cornmeal, because it has had the spoilable oily part of the seed removed, doesn't need to be kept refrigerated. Then again, it's less nutritious than whole-grain cornmeal. For baking purposes, the two are interchangeable.

Cornmeal adds both flavor and texture to breads, not to mention extra nutrition. Try experimenting with some in your favorite recipe. But stay away from an all-cornmeal formula. Without some wheat-based flour as a binder in the mix, your bread machine is likely to dispense hot crumbs — tasty hot crumbs, I'll grant you, but crumbs nonetheless.

Another flavorsome and nutritious addition to bread is oats. Oats are, or at least were for a very long time, the mainstay of Scottish sustenance. Despite Samuel Johnson's definition of them as "a grain which in England is generally given to horses, but in Scotland supports the people" and my own childhood memories of the sticky porridge that appeared in my bowl at breakfast time at my aunt's and if not finished off reappeared at dinnertime fried, oats really are a tasty grain. There were simply times when folks had too many of them. Again harking back to Scotland, in olden days in that country there was a holiday called Oatmeal Monday, a midterm celebration at Scottish universities when fathers of the poorer students would traditionally bring them a. sack of oats to nourish them for the remainder of the term.

In the guise of oatmeal, oats are used both in and on top of breads as well as for cereal. But oats come in other sizes and shapes. There are oat groats, the cleaned and hulled whole grain, and then there are cracked oats and steel-cut oats, the latter being groats diced up by sharp steel blades. Because no heat is generated in this process, it is reputed to retain more of the flavor and nutrition of the groats. All these coarser versions of the cereal add texture and emphasis as well as flavor to an oaten bread.

Semolina, milled from protein-rich durum wheat with only the bran layer removed, will be found listed in some of the recipes in this book, along with barley, millet, and amaranth, cousin of the colorful cockscomb planted in many an annual flower garden. These are all nutritious additions to bread. The more familiar wheat germ and wheat bran can enrich a blander flour as well.

The grains have always dominated European and American bread baking. But flours made from potatoes, beans, and other legumes have often been used to supplement the more traditional flours. In earlier times, these admixtures were for the most part instances of manifest adulteration, the grain flours up until a century ago being reasonably expensive, while flour from other sources could often be had at a cheaper price.

Sometimes, however, the blending of different flours produced a genuinely more wholesome commodity. An outstanding example of such a loaf is Ezekiel bread, a recipe for which will be found among the multigrains. Another is the rich, baking-powder-leavened teff nut bread.

Potatoes make for a heavenly light loaf, as a good Hungarian potato bread will testify. Buckwheat, a relative of rhubarb, better known to some in its hulled and cooked form, kasha, lends a loaf distinctive robustness. Seeds like sunflower and flaxseed contribute a piquancy both visually attractive and very nutritious.

Eggs add extra protein to a bread, and their yolks add color. Eggs also help the dough to rise. Their leavening is a physical effect, based on the swelling of the whites, where other leavening agents work their magic by means of a chemical reaction, releasing carbon dioxide.

Egg-based breads usually need more oil or butter than might otherwise be called for, to keep from drying out. Loaves rich in egg tend to go stale rather quickly. But in the unlikely event that you have leftovers of such loaves, they make great bread puddings.

Besides the extra shortening, extra salt is needed in egg breads, to counteract their natural blandness. On the whole, I don't use much salt in my loaves, which is why a taste range is given for that seasoning in the recipes. Susan was put on a low-salt diet when carrying our first child some twenty years ago, and between that and numerous years of pureeing items from the day's menu for baby food, we've never gone back to a heavy hand with the salt shaker. Nevertheless, salt affects bread in more ways than taste. It enhances the effectiveness of the gluten in the flour, helping to loft the dough. It also keeps the dough from rising too fast and then collapsing.

However, if you come across an old recipe for salt-rising bread, don't assume from the name that such bread used no yeast. The dough for salt-rising bread was kept warm and expanding in a container of heated rock salt; in those cozy environs the wild yeasts did their thing.

Yeast is the most common leavening agent used in bread making. It is available in fresh form as cake yeast, dried under the name active dry yeast, and in a new so-called rapid-rise version. The recipes in this book all call for active dry yeast. Cake yeast is not readily proofed and dispersed throughout a dough mixed and rested in a baking machine, while rapid-rise yeast will often cause the dough to overflow the pan before the end of the machine's allotted resting cycle and ooze into a real mess around the heating coils.

Yeasts are one-celled, naturally occurring wild plants that multiply incredibly rapidly, given the right conditions. Those conditions include warmth, moisture, and carbohydrates. The first of these is supplied by the bread machine's diminutive oven, the last by the flour and, often, sugar. The trick is to balance the proportions of flour, sweeteners, and liquids to achieve a blend the yeast can work with.

Provided with these necessities, the yeast initiates a fermentation process the by-product of which is carbon dioxide gas. The gas becomes ensnared in the fabric of the dough, and the gluten in the dough acts like spandex, stretching into miniballoons full of carbon dioxide. Once the bread has begun to bake, the fermentation stops, arrested by the penetrating heat. But the bubbles remain. They are what give bread its familiar porous texture.

While domesticated yeast is the primary leavener in homemade breads today, it wasn't always so. Sourdough was the mainstay of bread making in pioneer days, and some of the starters passed on from generation to generation came to this country from the Old

World, hoarded carefully on the long transatlantic voyages by settlers from Europe. Sourdough remains alive and well today, and is regaining favor among bread aficionados. But it is, remember, a wild thing. A bit different from the other leaveners, sourdough and its care have a chapter to themselves.

Baking soda and baking powder were also much-used leaveners in earlier days, especially when the warmth, time, and tending that yeast breads required were scarce. Baking soda is the oldest chemical leavening agent around. It is traditionally combined with acidic liquids like buttermilk in a recipe. Being alkaline, the baking soda reacts with the acid in these liquids to produce carbon dioxide. The reaction is a very quick one, which is why these breads have traditionally been rushed from the batter bowl to a preheated oven.

But there's no way to rush the current generation of bread machines, so pure baking-soda breads do not fare well in these devices. Adding extra baking soda to a recipe in an attempt to boost the gas output doesn't work.

Traditional baking powder is a combination of baking soda and cream of tartar, an acid. Double-acting baking powder, the only kind available commercially today, uses calcium phosphate and sodium aluminum sulfate as its acids. The term "double-acting" refers to the fact that this powder releases gas twice, once when it comes in contact with moisture, a second time when heated. It is the fact that it produces carbon dioxide on heating, which baking soda by itself does not do, that makes baking powder utilizable in a bread machine.

Like sourdough, baking powder has a way with a loaf distinctively its own, as you will see — and taste — whenever working with it. The chapter devoted to baking-powder, or quick, breads contains a number of exceptionally tasty loaves raised with the help of this riser. But cultivated yeast remains the monarch of the leavening world.

The fermentable sugar that boosts the growth of baker's yeast in many bread recipes can come from a variety of sources. White sugar, brown sugar, molasses, corn syrup, maple syrup, honey, even barley malt — all have their place in bread making. Each adds a slightly different taste to a loaf, all add tenderness to it as well, and all can normally be substituted one for the other, although not necessarily on a one-to-one basis. Don't be afraid to experiment.

Almost anything can go into a loaf of bread, and nowhere is this more true than when it comes to the liquids that can be pressed into service. Cider's been used; so has tea, notably in Irish currant bread. The broth left from cooking vegetables substitutes nicely for the water or other liquid called for in a recipe, adding both extra nourishment and extra flavor. Such broths have a natural affinity with herb, vegetable, and savory breads.

Where you substitute a broth for milk in a recipe, you do need to know that the resulting loaf will not be quite as soft and tightly grained as the milk loaf would be. Milk breads are exceptionally tender.

Whole milk and skim milk can be used interchangeably in almost all of the recipes in this book. I happen to prefer the whole; it gives a richer, softer crumb. But skim milk can usually be substituted for it with no real loss in flavor and very little loss in texture.

In general, water makes a crust crisper and the loaf inside chewier than milk does. Milk browns the crust and adds tenderness and keeping quality. Buttermilk does the same, only better. You'll find it a common ingredient in quick-bread recipes, because its acidity sets off the requisite reaction in baking soda and baking powder.

Cream, sour cream, cottage cheese, and yogurt are other dairy products prized for their tenderizing role in bread making. I often use a dollop of nonfat dry milk for added flavor and nourishment in a loaf calling for water as its liquid. Noninstant powdered dry milk is even more nourishing, because it has not been heated as much as the instant variety during the drying process. However, it has a tendency to form lumps unless whipped into the water before being mixed with flour. It is also not as readily available as the common nonfat instant variety.

Butter is by today's fitness standards a naughty little richness sometimes occurring in bread. But it does serve a function, helping the dough to stretch and making the yeast's leavening task easier. It also makes for a moister, richer-tasting loaf. I use unsalted butter; it's reputed to blend more smoothly with other ingredients than salted butter does. Of course, with a bread machine everything gets thrown around in the mixing and agitating cycle, so I'm not sure if that point carries the value it once did. In any case, if what you have around your house is salted butter, don't put off your baking on that account. Simply adjust the amount of plain salt you use in a given recipe accordingly.

Oil has greater cachet than butter in many circles these days. If you are on a restricted cholesterol intake, you can substitute canola oil for butter. It will work in the recipes in this book with only a minor loss in taste. Also you'll find a number of the recipes calling for olive oil, which imparts its own bit of flavor while at the same time being right for the cholesterol-conscious. Incidentally, a small but nifty tip comes to mind in connection with using oil in bread making: where a recipe calls for both oil and a gooey sweetener such as molasses, if you measure out the oil first, the syrup will slide out of the same spoon or cup cleanly.

Lecithin, which you'll note in a few of the recipes included in this book, is a natural phosphatide, or phospholipid, derived from soybeans, corn, egg yolk, and other sources. It acts as an emulsifier and wetting agent, facilitating the mixing of ingredients and, in the case of bread, interacting with the gluten found in flour to add elasticity and leavening power to the dough. It particularly helps solid whole-grain breads to rise. Most health-food stores carry it.

The health-food stores and alternative-lifestyle purveyors are also good sources for the occasional odd ingredient like flaxseed or a specialty flour not available at the supermarket. Other sources for ingredients you might not have on hand are listed at the back of this book.

3 · Tips and Tricks for Electronic Baking

NONE OF MY REGULAR BREAD PANS have bucket-hoop handles like the ones on bread machine pans. This would be no big deal were it not for the fact that the unaccustomed hoop provides such an inviting handhold. Even when grasping the pan with potholders, one is prone to grab the hoop with a bare hand absentmindedly on occasion — at least I am, as my mildly burned fingertips will attest. Apart from that all too repeatable learning experience, one soon adjusts to the differences between traditional baking and its bread machine counterpart.

Differences there are, though. Consider, for instance, the order in which the ingredients are mixed. The sequence varies even from machine to machine.

The instructions for some bread machines specify that the liquids are to be measured into the pan first, then the solids, then the yeast. This particular sequence is presumably designed to keep the yeast from percolating down into the liquids at the bottom of the pan and being activated by the moisture too soon. But that becomes a real peril only when you are setting the timer to mobilize the machine at some future point. If your bread is to be baked in the ordinary course of events, such restraining measures aren't needed.

The directions supplied with other machines state that you are to put the yeast in the pan first, a little bit in each corner, then cover it with the solid ingredients, pouring the liquids in last. What reasoning lies behind this order, I'm not sure.

The problem of where and when to add the yeast is solved very neatly where a machine has a separate yeast dispenser. The leavening is simply added there after all the other ingredients have been placed in the baking pan. This dispenser can also be used for baking powder. But in that case you have to be supercareful not to pack the powder down in the slightest. Baking powder is very fine; it does not flow as readily as the granular yeast for which the dispenser was designed. On the whole, I find it safer to put the baking powder right in with the other ingredients when making quick breads, even in a machine with a yeast dispenser.

This might be the place to mention two things to be remembered about bread machines. First, they are Japanese in origin, and Japan's traditional cuisine is not bread-based. Although the Japanese like bread, it is a relatively new and foreign commodity. Part of its popularity probably stems from this very fact. However, because bread does not have a long cultural heritage in those islands, the breads assimilated do not have the broad range of ingredients, textures, and flavor taken for granted in European-based cultures. The second thing to remember is that while bread machines may be turning Japan into the land of the rising yeast, they were designed by engineers, not bakers. The combination of these two factors perhaps explains why the manufacturers' recipe booklets tucked in with the machines seem so mundane and repetitive.

Bread machines are capable of far more than the monotonous examples of culinary art presented in the makers' brochures. But you do have to experiment, sometimes modifying both the ingredients and the mixing sequence given in traditional recipes to the logistics of the machine. For instance, you can't simply toss a little more flour into the dough during kneading when it just doesn't feel right.

Sometimes what's needed is a simple alteration in the manufacturer's instructions on placing ingredients in your machine. For example, when baking a heavy loaf such as a pumpernickel or a rye or one using buttermilk, sour cream, and other dense liquids, you may end up with a half-baked mess the consistency of custard topped by caked flour. What has happened in this case is that, because the engineering considerations involved in designing a mixing blade that will pull easily out of a finished loaf conflict with the scientific principles of mixing and agitation, the machine has failed to blend and knead the ingredients properly. It's been doing what's known in the propeller industry as cavitating, the blade carving out an air-filled void in the material surrounding it and then spinning rapidly with reduced efficiency.

You can achieve approximately the same sorry results by failing to put the mixing blade back in the pan after washing those two components. That's something I did more than once at the beginning of my adventure with bread machines, if only because putting something in the bottom of a pan is so counterintuitive to someone accustomed to regular baking pans.

At any rate, if you end up with unincorporated flour lining the top or outer edges of your loaves, try reversing the order of the ingredients, adding the liquids last. Don't attempt this in a recipe you are planning to use with the overnight timer unless your machine has a separate yeast dispenser; the yeast would certainly be activated too soon. Then again, the culprit in a cavitating bread machine is usually a dough heavy in eggs or milk products, and because of possible spoilage, you wouldn't be letting such a dough sit overnight anyhow.

Another remedy for cavitation may be to alter the consistency of the dough you're working with to suit your machine better. The design of a bread machine's baking pan is such that most doughs should, after some mixing and machine kneading, form a ball around the blending blade. This ball will then run around the edges of the pan picking up extra bits of flour and other ingredients that may have temporarily clung to the nonstick walls. When you've heard the dough being agitated for quite a while during the first kneading, take a peek and see if the ball of dough is forming. It's perfectly all right to lift the lid of a bread machine and sneak a look at what's happening inside during the preliminary kneading cycle, even though the manual will warn you against it. I peek all the time. I just don't do it later in the bread-making cycle, when the bread might be rising, and certainly not when it's actually baking — except for the one time when I burned my nose.

A dough that is too soft to form a ball will sometimes fail to pick up all the flour from the edges of the pan. Typically, a loaf that emerges from your electronic oven with a swirly pattern on top is telling you that your particular machine had a problem mixing that particular batter. This is not an uncommon occurrence when one is first trying out a recipe for a soft, moist, milk-based bread or working with a sticky dough like that for teff or rice bread. A little extra flour will often firm up the dough and improve the final results.

If, conversely, you find when you slice open a finished loaf that the ingredients are not evenly dispersed, the next time you try the recipe, add a bit more liquid than it calls for. Some variations in loaf density are due to the composition of the flour used, which differs from brand to brand and even from harvest to harvest within the same brand.

Bread machines do have their idiosyncrasies, just as conventional ovens do, and even identical ingredients used with the very same recipe may result in different loaves. As a general rule, however, you can count on white breads and doughs rich in eggs to rise the most, heavy ryes and corn or bran breads the least.

This doesn't mean that you should double a recipe to get a full-sized loaf. I've tried that, mostly to my sorrow. Some breads simply don't rise to the top of the pan in a bread machine. Early on in my exploration of bread machines, I tried to make a full-sized corn bread — and laid an egg. What I achieved was a large golden loaf with a raw oval blob in the middle. The baking cycle of the machines is such that the heat of their ovens cannot penetrate the center of so large and solid a loaf long enough to bake it properly.

While my trial-and-error adventures with doubling recipes ended in disaster, other innovations in bread making with a machine proved quite workable. I've tried any number of concoctions, including simply dumping a chocolate and a date-nut box-cake mix along with the requisite egg and water into the baking pan to see what the machine would do with them. The results were certainly on par with conventionally baked box cakes. Once I even dumped some leftover spaghetti into the pan with some oregano, basil, and garlic powder, thinking to make an Italian loaf; that particular endeavor was voted out of this book by my family.

At one point Revell, our ten-year-old son, proposed adding M&Ms or Skittles to a batch of bread I was making. I objected that the hard candy might scratch the pan's nonstick finish.

"Then why not Froot-Loops bread," teased our daughter Genevieve, nine years his senior. I was saved only by Revell's "Oh, dis-*gust*ing!"

Conventional or experimental, most breads bake well in a bread machine set to its quick, or short, cycle. Baking-powder breads, in fact, will usually work only if baked quickly. On the other hand, solid loaves like rye and blue-cheese breads generally need the long full cycle, to give the leavening time to raise the dough as much as possible.

Light, medium, or dark settings for loaf color are pretty much up to the individual baker. With rare exceptions, I use whatever setting the machine itself selects automatically when it's turned on. Known in computerese as the default setting, this is what the manufacturer has deemed the most-often-used selection.

As to which of all the bread machines works the best, the answer to that depends largely on the features you're looking for. Someday a machine somewhere will incorporate them all. Meanwhile, you'll need to decide which ones are most important to you.

Right now, some of the baking machines have a window that lets you see how a loaf is progressing; others do not. Some beep at you; some beep and flash at you. Some have a separate yeast dispenser, which assures that the yeast will not come in contact with any liquids until the proper time for it to do so.

Eventually, I hope, the machines will have a similar separate compartment for additions like raisins, dates, nuts, and so on. As things stand now, these ingredients tend to become a bit mashed during the prolonged kneading cycle. Certain machines do have a special beeper that can be set to signal the end of the mixing cycle, when such ingredients can more safely be added in the expectation that they will remain whole and unbroken. But a beeper doesn't work for me. Invariably I've stepped out of the kitchen for just a minute when those three little beeps have sounded the "add now" signal, and my raisin bread has remained raisinless and my nut bread has baked without the nuts. Besides, what if I hadn't been home? With a release compartment for the raisins and the nuts like that for yeast, the breads could make themselves all by themselves while I was gone.

One improvement I seriously hope future bread machines incorporate is some better means of access for cleaning. This would allow me to be even bolder than I am in my baking experiments, no longer daunted by the prospect of scraping out the burned remains of some failed dough from heating coils deep within the machine.

Speaking of cleaning, it is possible to glaze and garnish a loaf of bread without removing it from the machine, and I've done it that way, but some of the glaze usually dribbles down between the bread and the sides of the pan to sizzle into a sticky mess, and some of the seeds or other embellishments always bounce off and fall into the machine. Adding glazes and toppings in situ is, as things now stand, asking for trouble; and so I dutifully remove the loaves, add the finishing touches I envision as appropriate, and return them to the bread baker to bake on. But the nice thing about bread machines is supposed to be their convenience. I guess I shouldn't fault them for small failures; however, a design that facilitated cleaning would be an appreciable timesaver.

In the way of components, some bread machines come with a thicker baking pan than others do. The thicker pan seems to me to make better bread. Loaves appear to bake less evenly in the thinner pans, and often they have a disproportionately thick bottom crust.

Day-to-day fluctuations in temperature, the vicissitudes of altitude and atmosphere, variations in flour quality — such things can all affect the loft and lightness and uniformity of a loaf. When the photography for the jacket of this book was scheduled, for some inexplicable reason all the loaves I baked insisted, for three days running, on coming out of the pan slightly lopsided! Yet, overall, bread machines turn out consistently good, tasty loaves.

Whatever the bread you bake, when it comes from the oven hot and fragrant, your final task is to get the loaf out of its pan. Rapping the pan on the side of the counter helps, although the loaf still will not slide out quite as easily as one from a regular bread pan, as the beater in the bottom of a bread machine pan is loath to let its loaf go. Twiddling the screw at the bottom of the pan a few times — wearing an oven mitt — helps here.

Once the loaf is free, let it rest on a rack to cool for ten to twenty minutes before slicing it. Otherwise the retained steam will make your slices sticky. That wait, as the aroma of fresh-baked bread fills the room so irresistibly, may be the hardest part of baking with a bread machine.

4 · Basic Breads and Toast

IT WAS TOAST that first sold me on the idea of a bread machine. Oh, I'll grant, I'm enough of a baking enthusiast that I'll try almost anything, from a wild South Pacific yeast to a new long-handled Danish spring whisk, at least once. But to my mind there was something not quite proper about a bread machine. Even the combination of words making up the name clashed, both with each other and with the image of a cozy, sunny kitchen with a wood stove and a calico cat dozing on the warming shelf that the making of home-baked bread conjures up. All the same, the temptation of fresh toast every morning was real and undeniable.

All of the basic breads presented here make great toast. Some of the recipes in this section call for more than one type of flour, and readers may wonder why they have been put here rather than with the other multigrain breads. Certain flours are very solid, and some quite strong in taste; rye is an outstanding example. Breads using these flours often need the balance of a less dense constituent, hence the mix. But those associated with a particular grain are still thought of as the basic bread of that type in that they are staples, which is why they are included here.

Basic White Bread

Here's a lofty, light loaf of bread that those guarding against cholesterol can enjoy guilt-free. It's superior to store-bought diet bread, yet it contains none of the shortening usually associated with a tasty bread.

A quarter of a cup of toasted sesame seeds or a couple of teaspoonfuls of caraway seeds will add a delicious extra burst of flavor to the loaf. But don't attempt to use the Japanese black sesame seeds. Sprinkled over the top of the bread as it comes hot from the oven, they can add striking color contrast. Mix them into the dough, however, as I once did, and you'll have blue-black bread. It might taste fine, but somehow or other blue-black bread is aesthetically unacceptable.

> 1 cup water
> ¼ cup toasted sesame or 2 teaspoons
>   caraway seeds (optional)
> 2 cups unbleached all-purpose flour
> 1 tablespoon nonfat dry milk
> 2 tablespoons sugar
> ¼ to 1 teaspoon salt to taste
> 1½ teaspoons active dry yeast

Pour the water into the baking pan of your bread machine, unless the instructions for your machine specify that the leavening is to be placed in the pan first and the liquid last, and add the sesame or caraway seeds if desired. Then add the flour, dry milk, sugar, salt, and yeast. In machines equipped with a separate dispenser for the leavening, the yeast should be added to the dispenser after all the other ingredients have been placed in the pan.

A quick bake cycle can be used with this bread.

Basic All-Whole-Wheat Bread

W hen you combine the proteins of grain with those of dairy products, you create more complete food proteins, balanced like those of meat and fish. In a loaf such as this one, the whole-wheat grain and the buttermilk together provide a source of protein and fiber more acceptable than animal protein to many in today's fat-conscious culture. So here's a balanced loaf that should be as healthy as it is tasty.

> *1 cup buttermilk*
> *1 tablespoon unsulphured molasses*
> *1 tablespoon unsalted butter or canola*
> *   oil*
> *2½ cups whole-wheat flour*
> *2 tablespoons nonfat dry milk*
> *¼ to 1 teaspoon salt to taste*
> *1½ teaspoons active dry yeast*

Remember that if the instructions that came with your bread machine call for the yeast to be placed in the baking pan first, the dry ingredients should be added before the liquids. Otherwise put the buttermilk, molasses, and butter or canola oil in the pan, add the flour, dry milk, salt, and, if the instructions for your machine so direct, the yeast. If your machine has a separate dispenser for leavening, spoon the yeast into the dispenser after all the other ingredients have been measured into the baking pan.

Set the machine to its full bake cycle for this bread.

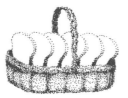

Light Whole-Wheat Bread

All the publicity over the healthfulness of whole grains and fiber aside, if you've spent your entire life eating white bread, then, let's face it, the darker varieties are going to take some getting used to. Nowhere is this more true than among children, whose sensitive taste buds and peer-pressure-prone personalities are apt to find Twinkies the ultimate in lunch-box fare. Well, here's a light whole-wheat bread that you might be able to slip them without their noticing.

The recipe produces an attractive tall loaf. It's a good summer bread that, toasted, accommodates the traditional ingredients of a BLT sandwich magnificently.

> 1 1/4 cups water
> 1 teaspoon honey
> 2 cups unbleached all-purpose flour
> 1/2 cup whole-wheat flour
> 1/2 cup uncooked oatmeal (not instant)
> 1/4 to 1 teaspoon salt to taste
> 1 1/2 teaspoons active dry yeast

Pour the water into the baking pan of your bread machine and add the spoonful of honey, followed by the all-purpose and whole-wheat flours, the oatmeal, salt, and yeast. Remember, however, to follow the directions that came with your particular machine for incorporating the leavening; if the yeast is to be placed in the pan first thing, then the water and honey should be reserved till last.

Use either the regular or the quick cycle on your machine for baking this loaf.

Basic Rye Bread

Rye bread, that tasty European staple from the oven, is one of those tricky loaves that often fail to meet the expectations of the home baker. The first loaf I made, a decade ago, would still be sitting around if Susan hadn't finally disposed of it. My plan had been to drill three holes in it, providing it with a possible use as a bowling ball.

The recipe that follows makes a nice firm loaf. Because of this, the bread will be about half as tall as some of the lighter, more delicate loaves whose recipes are found in this book, so don't be overcome with disappointment when you pull the pan out and have to peer over the edge to see the bread. Once you've sampled it, you'll love its dense, fine-grained, moist texture.

The instant coffee you'll notice among the ingredients is for color. Old-time rye-bread recipes often called for Postum, a toasted grain-based coffee substitute that can still be used instead of the coffee if preferred and if it's handy. My hunch regarding the origin of this ingredient as a coloring agent in the bread is that, somewhere back in history, one baker or another added some accidentally blackened, burned grain to his loaves rather than simply throwing it out, and the sumptuous-looking darkened loaves became objects of preference. Whatever the case, the dark rye bread you see at the local bakery also has one coloring agent or another added to give it a look of richness.

When slicing loaves fresh from a bread machine, one tends to go for substance, both because it can be tricky to cut thin slices from them and because one doesn't ordinarily want wimpy slices of a good bread anyhow. But this particular rye bread really should be cut into slices no thicker than an eighth to three-sixteenths of an inch across, and it stands up well to such delicate carving.

The bread is superb with sliced hard-boiled eggs and anchovies, a flavorful cheese like Brie or Swiss, watercress and mayonnaise, or sliced cucumbers and butter. Make a whole trayful of small open-faced sandwiches from it for a delightful summer meal.

1¼ cups buttermilk
2 tablespoons olive oil
1 tablespoon dehydrated minced onion
1 cup unbleached all-purpose flour
1 cup rye flour
1 cup whole-wheat flour
¼ cup firmly packed dark brown sugar
1 tablespoon instant coffee, regular or
    decaffeinated, or Postum
1 tablespoon caraway seeds
½ to 1 teaspoon salt to taste
1½ teaspoons active dry yeast

Unless the instructions that came with your bread machine call for starting with the yeast, in which case you will need to remember to reverse the order in which you add the liquid and the dry ingredients, pour the buttermilk and olive oil into your baking pan and add the onion to soak for a minute or two while you assemble the other ingredients. The buttermilk bath will help to protect the nonstick surface of the baking pan from being scratched by the rather sharp-edged dehydrated onions when the batter is kneaded. Then add the all-purpose, rye, and whole-wheat flours, the brown sugar, coffee or Postum, caraway seeds, and salt. Last, add the yeast, following the instructions given for your particular machine. If the model you have features a separate dispenser for leavening, add the yeast there.

Set the machine on its regular full cycle to bake this loaf.

Basic Oatmeal Bread

Oatmeal bread always brings to my mind the Irish. Why that is I'm not exactly sure, since I associate the cereal itself more with the frugal Scots. The Scots make their porridge from the cracked but unflattened grain rather than from the paper-thin rolled oat flakes to which we are accustomed.

Whatever its original nationality, oatmeal bread is undeniably hearty and flavorful. The recipe given here makes a fine-textured, nutty, golden loaf. The use of bread flour instead of plain unbleached flour is helpful in this instance, giving the loaf more loft. But in any case, don't expect a really tall loaf. The bread will be nicely rounded on top, but rather squarish. What it lacks in height it will make up for in taste.

> 1 cup milk, whole or skim
> 2 tablespoons unsalted butter or
>   canola oil
> 2 cups bread flour
> 1 cup uncooked oatmeal (not in-
>   stant)
> 2 tablespoons dark brown sugar
> 1/4 to 1 teaspoon salt to taste
> 1 1/2 teaspoons active dry yeast
>
> GLAZE
>   1 egg white
>   2 tablespoons milk, whole or skim
>   oat flakes for garnish

Remember to follow the instructions for placement of the yeast provided with the specific model of bread machine that you have. Put the cupful of milk and the butter or canola oil in the baking pan first, unless directed to reserve the liquids till last, and add the flour, oatmeal, brown sugar, salt, and yeast.

Use either your machine's regular or its quick bake cycle for this bread. When you remove the finished loaf from its pan, while it's still piping hot, quickly whip together the egg white and the two tablespoons of milk and brush this glaze over the top of the hot bread. Either a pastry brush or the more traditional goose feather used in Ireland will do a fine job of this. Sprinkle the dome of the loaf liberally with oat flakes. Some will always fall off. Not to worry. Return the loaf to the pan and the pan to its baking slot in the machine. The oat flakes will cling firmly as the glaze cooks on from the retained heat of the bread and the oven and then cools, imparting the distinctive traditional look that makes oatmeal bread instantly recognizable.

Basic All-Semolina Bread

Semolina flour is ordinarily used in the making of pasta. Milled from protein-rich durum wheat with only the bran layer removed, the flour is creamy in color and grainy in texture, rather reminiscent of cornmeal. It makes a rich-looking, great-tasting bread.

Most grocery stores and supermarkets do not carry semolina flour. But just about every health-food store does. The flour is also often available in ethnic markets, particularly Italian and Middle Eastern ones. In the latter it will be found along with the coarser grind used for that region's justly acclaimed couscous.

The recipe given here produces a moist, fine-textured yellow loaf. It's a superlative toasting bread that goes particularly well with coarse-cut English marmalade.

1 cup buttermilk
1 egg

1 tablespoon unsalted butter or
  canola oil
2½ cups semolina flour
¼ to 1 teaspoon salt to taste
1½ teaspoons active dry yeast

Unless the instructions that came with your bread machine call for starting with the yeast, in which case you will need to reverse the order in which the liquid and the dry ingredients are incorporated into the batter, pour the buttermilk into your baking pan, break in the egg, and add the butter or canola oil. Then measure in the flour, salt, and yeast. If you have a machine with its own dispenser for leavening, add the yeast there.

Use a regular full baking cycle for this loaf.

Milk Bread

One of my most memorable meals ever was an early-morning one in Braunau am Inn served on a balcony overlooking the Austrian Alps. The day was postcard-picture perfect, sunny and sufficiently warm for comfort but still cool enough to make the steam rising from my generously sized cup of hot chocolate clearly visible. The hot chocolate came with a basket of small, fresh rolls, among which were some deliciously tender milk breads.

The larger milk loaf, similar to challah, resulting from the recipe given here achieves its sunny yellow appearance through the addition of eggs. The dough is so soft and sticky that it could never be kneaded by hand, so in effect what you have here is a soft, golden loaf that only a bread machine can make. The three eggs, incidentally, raise the volume of ingredients to very nearly the maximum that most bread machines can handle, which is one reason why the recipe calls for less yeast than usual.

½ cup milk, whole or skim
1 tablespoon dark corn syrup
3 eggs
3 tablespoons unsalted butter
2 cups unbleached all-purpose flour
¼ to ½ teaspoon salt to taste
1 teaspoon active dry yeast

GLAZE
   1 egg
   1 tablespoon cold water
   poppy seeds for garnish

Measure the milk and corn syrup into your baking pan, break the eggs into the liquids, and add the butter, cutting it into small chunks if it's not soft, as otherwise, since you're using a relatively large amount, it may not blend altogether evenly into the dough. Next measure in the flour and salt. Distribute the yeast according to the instructions given for the particular bread machine you have.

Use a quick bake cycle and, if available, a light loaf setting for this loaf. As soon as it has finished baking, take it from the machine and remove it gently from its pan. Beat the egg and cold water together for the glaze, brush this mixture over the dome of the loaf with a pastry brush, and sprinkle it with poppy seeds. Then ease the bread gently back into the pan, pop it back into the machine, and close the lid. The residual heat will bake the glaze on within a minute or two. Pull the pan out once more and remove the loaf, carefully so as not to dislodge the poppy seeds, to a rack to cool.

Sour Cream Bread

Here's a loaf that uses no liquids in the traditional sense, just sour cream for moisture. My original recipe for this bread called for water as well. But that version, when attempted in my machine, demonstrated quite graphically why bread machines should be designed for easier cleaning. It was smoke-alarm time.

This is not to discourage experimentation. I simply dropped the water from the recipe altogether and ended up with a soft, moist, white bread with a lovely puffed crown.

The loaf is perfect for French toast, its open texture holding the butter and pools of syrup delectably.

1 cup sour cream
2½ cups unbleached all-purpose flour
1 tablespoon dark brown sugar
¼ to 1 teaspoon salt to taste
1½ teaspoons active dry yeast

Scoop the sour cream into your baking pan and add the flour, brown sugar, and salt. Position the yeast according to the directions given for your machine, unless you have a machine with its own dispenser for leavening, in which case the yeast should be measured into the dispenser the very last thing.

A quick bake cycle gives the best results with this recipe.

5 · Multigrain Breads

 Even the most basic of breads often contain several different flours. But the recipes in this chapter encompass a broader spectrum of grains. Cornell bread, for instance, formulated by Dr. Clive McCay of the university of that name, was originated to return nourishment to the staff of life for people raised to believe in sliced white fluff as the only socially acceptable bread. The cut-oats and flaxseed bread recipes acknowledge the trend today toward including tasty, uncrushed seeds in bread. Ezekiel bread, well, do try it. It's an unusual delicacy.

Cornell Bread

Today's emphasis on nutrition and flavor in bread suggests that it might be time to take another look at what some readers may remember as "the Cornell formula." Not much has been heard of it lately, but its value is far from spent.

For centuries bread was the staff of life. For centuries it was also an emblem of social stature. Dark, rich bread betokened peasantry; white, bland bread denoted a high social plane.

But increasing wealth in the wake of the industrial revolution and the development of mechanized baking together conspired to put white bread in the baskets of even the poor, and the rank it symbolized within their grasp. The sad corollary was that those who depended on bread for their very subsistence were robbed of its sustenance.

The so-called enriched flours of the twentieth century have all the wheat germ removed from them, because the germ makes the grain hard to mill and the flour hard to keep. True, a few nutrients from the original germ are restored to the flour after milling, but the result is still far less nutritious than even the finest of white flours in the days before modern milling.

In an effort to counter malnutrition among the underprivileged and the institutionalized of America, who earlier in this century lived on bread to a degree inconceivable today, a bread mix designed to deliver more nutrition in white bread was developed at Cornell University. To the processed wheat flour were added nonfat dry milk, soy flour, and wheat germ. Cornell bread had everything going for it: it was inexpensive, it was nourishing, and it was white.

Today's national dietary abundance has given priority to eating less rather than to getting enough to eat, and Cornell bread has fallen into oblivion. However, it is still a nutritious loaf, and one that the undernourished of the present generation, the Fluffernutter school set, take to as if it were, well, white bread.

The Cornell mix can be purchased by mail from some of the suppliers listed in the back of this book. You can also make your own, using the formula below.

BASIC CORNELL FLOUR MIX

1 tablespoon soy flour
1 tablespoon wheat germ
1 tablespoon nonfat dry milk
unbleached all-purpose or bleached
white flour

Mix the soy flour, wheat germ, and dry milk in the bottom of a measuring cup. Add enough regular all-purpose or white flour to make one full cup, and stir with a fork to blend.

By multiplying the ingredients proportionately, you can make up a large batch of this mix at one time. It will keep well if stored in an airtight container in your freezer. To make a loaf from it, measure out the amount of flour mix needed and let it reach room temperature before starting your dough.

The Cornell bread recipe given here produces an average-sized, nicely rounded loaf. Unassuming-looking, it nevertheless packs good flavor and nutrition under its modest crown.

> *1 cup milk, whole or skim*
> *2 tablespoons honey*
> *1 tablespoon unsalted butter or canola*
>   *oil*
> *2 cups Cornell mix*
> *¼ to 1 teaspoon salt to taste*
> *1½ teaspoons active dry yeast*

Pour the milk into the baking pan of your bread machine and add the honey, butter or canola oil, Cornell mix, and salt. Distribute the yeast as directed for your particular machine.

Bake on a quick cycle.

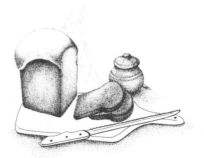

Four-Grains Breakfast Bread

Old-fashioned harvests of the fields are encountering an amazing revival in the grain-and-fiber-conscious nineties, particularly at breakfast time. Oatmeal, once plebeian, is suddenly in vogue. Bran muffins abound as never before. And ancient grains like amaranth and quinoa are in demand.

Unfortunately, the popularity of these edibles sometimes simply proves the power of fad over taste. However healthy they might be, certain of them have all the flavor of recycled cardboard.

But here's a loaf that packs the nutrition of four different grains and a whole lot of flavor besides. There's a hint of cinnamon in the air when it's baking.

The amaranth in the recipe includes among its benefits the amino acids lysine and methionine, elements largely absent in most other flours. High in fiber and rich in iron, it contains as much as 16 percent protein.

1 cup milk, whole or skim
1 tablespoon honey
1 egg
2 tablespoons unsalted butter or canola oil
1 teaspoon vanilla extract
1 cup unbleached all-purpose flour
½ cup semolina flour
½ cup amaranth flour
½ cup uncooked oatmeal (not instant)
1 teaspoon cinnamon
½ teaspoon ginger
¼ to 1 teaspoon salt to taste
1½ teaspoons active dry yeast

Pour the milk into your baking pan, unless the instructions that came with your bread machine call for starting with the yeast, in which case you will need to reverse the order in which the liquid and the dry ingredients are incorporated. Spoon the honey into the pan, break in the egg, and add the butter or canola oil and the vanilla extract. Then measure in the all-purpose, semolina, and amaranth flours and the oatmeal. Last, add the cinnamon, ginger, salt, and yeast. If your machine has a separate dispenser for leavening, the yeast should be placed there.

Use a quick bake cycle for this bread.

Seven-Grains Bread

Multigrain cereals in a wide variety of mixes are available at health-food stores and some supermarkets. The most popular of these blends is probably one version or another of the seven-grains mixture used here, an Arrowhead Mills mix of coarsely ground wheat, oats, triticale, millet, soybeans, buckwheat, and yellow corn.

A dense, textured bread has no equal as a foil for a good, sharp cheese or a flavorsome pâté, and it was in search of such a bread that I decided to try this combination of grains to vary a whole-wheat loaf I'd been baking for some time. The bread is sweeter than what one might expect from the addition of a mere quarter cup of honey, and, if you prefer, the honey can be omitted and an egg or just the white from a large egg can be used in its place. The loaf is also quite compact and square; for a somewhat lighter texture, 1½ cups of unbleached all-purpose flour can be substituted for 1½ cups of the whole-wheat flour.

> 1 cup seven-grains cereal
> 1½ cups boiling water
> ¼ cup honey or, if preferred,
>   1 egg or the white of 1 large egg

3 tablespoons olive oil
3 cups whole-wheat flour or 1½
    cups unbleached all-purpose
    flour and 1½ cups whole-
    wheat flour
½ to 1 teaspoon salt to taste
2 teaspoons active dry yeast

Put the seven-grains cereal mixture in the baking pan of your bread machine and pour the boiling water over it. Let the mush cool to the point where it feels merely warm before incorporating the other ingredients, unless your machine has a separate dispenser for the yeast, in which case no wait is necessary, since the yeast is not added to the dough for the first half hour or so of mixing. Next, add the honey or egg or egg white, the olive oil, the whole-wheat flour or all-purpose and whole-wheat flours combined, and the salt. Top it off with the yeast, unless directed otherwise in the instructions for your machine.

Bake on full cycle, using a medium setting for color if your machine permits this choice.

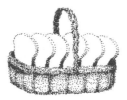

Steel-Cut Oat Bread

The heartiest breads usually contain some whole grain. But many of the cereals when left whole need to be softened before they are used in baking. Even steel-cut oats, which are the chopped version of this grain, are no exception. Accordingly, for this loaf you will need to allow an extra fifteen minutes, say, for the boiling water in which the cut oats are soaked to cool to the point where it will not inadvertently kill the leavening.

The recipe given here yields a loaf in which the steel-cut oats are so scattered that one's teeth and taste buds come upon them with pleasant surprise rather than jaded familiarity. The bread makes a thoroughly satisfying meal in itself sliced into thick slabs slathered with butter and garnished with something crisp like sliced cucumbers or watercress.

> 1 cup steel-cut oats
> 1 1/2 cups boiling water
> 2 tablespoons unsulphured molasses
> 1 egg
> 2 cups unbleached all-purpose flour
> 1 cup rye flour
> 1/2 cup cornmeal
> 2 tablespoons nonfat dry milk
> 1/2 to 1 teaspoon salt to taste
> 1 1/2 teaspoons active dry yeast

Measure the oats into the baking pan of your bread machine and pour the boiling water over them. Let them stand until they are no more than warm to the touch before adding the other ingredients unless your machine has a separate dispenser for the yeast, as otherwise the hot liquid will kill the leavening. Spoon the molasses into the mush, break in the egg, and add the all-purpose and rye flours, the cornmeal, dry milk, salt, and, following the instructions given for your particular machine, the yeast.

Bake on full cycle.

Flaxseed Bread

Flaxseed is a rich source of protein, and this is a bread I developed early in my bread machine experiments for our daughter Genevieve, who is a vegetarian. The first couple of loaves I baked contained all whole-wheat flour, no white, as well as millet, a grand source of vitamins and minerals. They also boasted honey, garlic, and olive oil. I was striving for an all-around health loaf here.

Genevieve dutifully took a bite, chewed, and commented, "They actually gave you a recipe for this?"

"Well, no, I was experimenting."

With a smile that made me realize how truly beyond verbal description is the renowned expression of the Mona Lisa, she placed the slice, one bite missing, gently at the far edge of her butter plate.

Half a dozen modifications and simplifications later, the recipe included here evolved, and everyone liked the end result. The loaf is a squarish one unusual in flavor, good and crusty and distinctively flecked with the mahogany-colored flaxseed. Slices of it go particularly well, I've found, with liverwurst and thinly sliced onions or a delicately carved smoked ham, both combinations that rather contradict the original high-protein-vegetarian intent of the bread but that nevertheless make a delightful meal.

> 1/2 cup flaxseed
> 1 1/2 cups scalded milk, whole or skim,
>   still hot
> 3 tablespoons olive oil
> 1 1/2 cups unbleached all-purpose flour
> 1 1/2 cups whole-wheat flour
> 2 teaspoons dry mustard
> 1/2 to 1 teaspoon salt to taste
> 1 1/2 teaspoons active dry yeast

Put the flaxseed in your bread machine pan and cover with the hot milk. Let cool about fifteen minutes or until tepid before adding the other ingredients. Then measure in the olive oil, all-purpose and whole-wheat flours, dry mustard, and salt. Here as elsewhere, salt is very much a matter of individual taste, but this loaf seems to require a bit more than most to bring out its full flavor. Scatter the yeast over the dry ingredients, or spoon it into the yeast dispenser if your machine has one.

Use a regular full baking cycle for this bread.

Sunflower Bread

I n Sweden they make a sunflower-seed loaf called sunshine bread that uses apple cider as its liquid base. Cider can be substituted for the buttermilk in this recipe as well; it will give the loaf a fruitier bouquet. But, personally, I like the creamy texture the buttermilk lends the bread; somehow it complements perfectly the taste burst of the sunflower seeds.

Nutritious and flavorful, the sunflower seeds contribute contrast and interest besides, and they do so without the expense associated with those other celebrated providers of protein-rich sustenance, nuts. For a real treat, try slices of this bread with a smooth spreadable cheese like Brie or even a fragrant Limburger.

> *1 cup buttermilk or cider*
> *2 tablespoons olive oil*
> *1 tablespoon unsulphured molasses*
> *½ cup hulled sunflower seeds*
> *1½ cups unbleached all-purpose flour*
> *1½ cups whole-wheat flour*
> *¼ to 1 teaspoon salt to taste*
> *1½ teaspoons active dry yeast*

Pour the buttermilk or cider into the baking pan of your bread machine and spoon in the olive oil and molasses. Add the sunflower seeds, the all-purpose and whole-wheat flours, and the salt. Follow the directions that came with your particular machine for incorporating the yeast.

Use a quick cycle in baking this loaf.

Ezekiel Bread

Ezekiel bread is one of those exceptionally wholesome breads that sometimes result from the blending of a number of different and, in this case, somewhat unusual flours. The recipe, and its name, can be traced to a Biblical injunction found in Ezekiel 4:9: "Take thou also unto thee wheat, and barley, and beans, and lentils, and millet, and spelt, and put them in one vessel, and make thee bread thereof."

Simplifying the modern bread maker's life, at least one company I know of, King Arthur Flour, listed as a source in the back of the book, makes available a premixed Ezekiel flour. The blend does not include spelt, a primitive and not readily available wheat whose chaff does not separate from the grain in threshing. But considering this proclivity of the spelt toward clinging to the chaff, I'd suspect that a 100 percent Ezekiel mix would pack a lot of straw with it. I know fiber is a prized constituent in the diet of the au courant today, but enough is enough.

This speltless Ezekiel recipe produces a compact, nutty, slightly chewy loaf with a keeping quality better than that of many machine-baked breads.

> 1 cup buttermilk
> 1/4 cup honey
> 1 tablespoon olive oil
> 2 1/2 cups Ezekiel mix
> 1/4 to 1 teaspoon salt to taste
> 1 1/2 teaspoons active dry yeast

Pour the buttermilk, honey, and olive oil into the baking pan of your bread machine, add the Ezekiel mix, the salt, and, if the instructions for your machine so direct, the yeast. If your machine has a separate dispenser for leavening, spoon the yeast into the dispenser after all the other ingredients have been measured into the baking pan. Remember that if your machine has no separate dispenser and the yeast is to be placed in the pan first, the dry ingredients should be added next, before the liquids.

Bake on your machine's full cycle.

Anadama Bread

Most corn breads contain molasses, honey, buttermilk, or a combination of these ingredients, all of which are acidic and react with baking soda to activate its leavening power. Thus baking soda is the leavening agent traditionally used in making these breads. Anadama bread is an exception.

There are many versions of Anadama bread — almost as many as there are stories purporting to explain how the loaves' curious name came about. But what sets them all apart from the corn breads is the yeast used instead of baking soda to leaven them. The recipe given here makes a dense, nicely corn-flavored loaf. Like all corn bread, it is best eaten warm with butter and honey.

> *3/4 cup milk, whole or skim*
> *1/4 cup unsulphured molasses*
> *1 egg*
> *2 tablespoons unsalted butter or canola oil*
> *2 cups unbleached all-purpose flour*
> *1 cup cornmeal*
> *1/2 to 1 teaspoon salt to taste*
> *1 1/2 teaspoons active dry yeast*

Pour the milk and the molasses into your bread pan, break in the egg, and add the butter or canola oil, the flour, cornmeal, salt, and yeast. The leavening should be added according to the specific instructions given for your bread machine.

Bake this loaf on either a long or a short cycle, using a light color setting if your machine permits that choice.

Millet Cornmeal Bread

Millet is an ancient grain much used by the Romans, a fact my high-school Latin studies made memorable. The Romans mixed millet and wheat flours for their bread. But millet is an even more congenial complement of corn; added to a corn bread, the seeds, left whole, add crunchy bursts of extra flavor.

Revell, who keeps a bird feeder stocked with seed for the English sparrows, jays, cardinals, and other feathered friends that winter over on our farm, has suspected me of raiding his supplies on occasion for this loaf, but it's not true. I buy the millet from a local health-food store, where you will find it as well.

This recipe is another serendipitous exception to the rule of leavening cornmeal breads with baking soda or baking powder. Then again, it has a lot more than just cornmeal in it.

> 1 cup milk, whole or skim
> 1/4 cup honey
> 1 egg
> 2 tablespoons unsalted butter or canola
>   oil
> 1/2 cup millet seed
> 2 cups unbleached all-purpose flour
> 1 cup cornmeal
> 1/2 to 1 teaspoon salt to taste
> 1 1/2 teaspoons active dry yeast

Pour the milk and honey into the baking pan of your bread machine, break in the egg, and add the butter or canola oil, the millet, flour, cornmeal, salt, and yeast, following the directions that came with your machine for incorporating the leavening.

This loaf is best baked on your machine's regular cycle.

6 · Herb Breads

THERE'S NO AROMA from the kitchen more tempting than that of a freshly baked loaf of bread — unless it's that from a freshly baked loaf of herb bread. The combined fragrances of a rich yeasty dough and herbs like dill and caraway send the taste buds into a frenzy of anticipation.

Herb breads are a good place to dispose of broths left from cooking up vegetables. Herbs and vegetables have a natural affinity for each other, after all. And why use plain water for your bread when there's a tasty and nutritious broth sitting in the refrigerator? Just remember to take it out to reach room temperature before using, or warm it in a pan.

Casserole Batter Bread

This loaf, as its name implies, was originally baked in a casserole. That factor gives its traditional form a natural affinity to the rounded loaves produced in a bread machine. It's a nice soft loaf with a very even texture and a puffed crown. Considering the flavoring ingredients, I was not surprised when our kids took to spreading slices of it with tomato sauce and mozzarella and popping them into the toaster oven for a quick snack.

1 cup milk, whole or skim
2 tablespoons unsalted butter or canola
  oil
2½ cups unbleached all-purpose flour
2 tablespoons sugar
1 teaspoon dried basil
1 teaspoon dried oregano
½ teaspoon garlic powder or 1 clove of
  fresh garlic, pressed
¼ to 1 teaspoon salt to taste
1½ teaspoons active dry yeast

Put the milk and the butter or canola oil in the baking pan of your bread machine, add the flour, sugar, basil, oregano, garlic, and salt, then measure in the yeast, unless the instructions that came with your machine call for reversing the order in which the yeast and the milk and butter or oil are incorporated.

Bake on either the regular or the quick cycle of your machine, and prepare to sample a truly flavorsome bread.

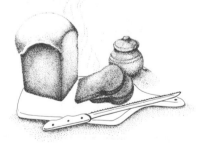

Dijon Rye Bread

Mustard and rye are two hearty tastes that go exceptionally well together. Their affinity inspired this bread, whose name derives from the type and origin of the mustard used, not from any ascribed birthplace of the loaf itself. I've never seen mustard rye bread in Dijon. On the other hand, I'm sure the epicurean sensibilities of that municipality's city fathers would not be offended by such a flavorful namesake.

By all means use a grainy version of the mustard for extra piquancy. For both visual and gustatory accent, add a mustard glaze. This bread makes a great accompaniment to spit-roasted chicken or a hearty bean soup.

> 1 cup water or vegetable broth
> 2 tablespoons olive oil
> 2 tablespoons unsulphured molasses
> ⅓ cup prepared Dijon mustard
> 1 cup unbleached all-purpose flour
> 1 cup whole-wheat flour
> 1 cup rye flour
> 1 tablespoon instant coffee, regular
>   or decaffeinated, or Postum
> ½ teaspoon dried thyme
> ½ to 1 teaspoon salt to taste
> 1½ teaspoons active dry yeast

> *GLAZE*
> 1 teaspoon prepared Dijon mustard
> 1 teaspoon molasses
> 1 teaspoon warm water

Pour the water or vegetable broth into the baking pan of your bread machine and add the oil, molasses, and mustard, unless the instructions for your machine specify that the yeast is to be placed in the bottom of the pan, followed by first the dry and then the liquid ingredients. Measure in the all-purpose, whole-wheat, and rye flours, the instant coffee or Postum, and the thyme, and salt. Add the yeast according to the directions for your particular machine.

Bake on full cycle. To glaze the loaf, mix together the teaspoonful of mustard, molasses, and warm water and, while the loaf is still hot from the pan, brush this mixture over its crown with a pastry brush. The glaze will cool to a rich gloss.

Pesto Bread

Maybe it was reading Dr. Seuss's *Green Eggs and Ham* to my children too many times, maybe it was the pestofication of so many dishes during the yuppie eighties, maybe it was the fact that an exceptionally gray winter was dragging, oh, so slowly into spring that I was actually longing to have a little green in my life again — whatever the case, one day I concocted a pesto bread.

Pestos are mixtures of herbs and/or other ingredients such as olives or sun-dried tomatoes blended with oil into a paste. Traditionally, their concoction involved the use of a mortar and pestle. Hence the name. Today, most pestos are made in a blender or a food processor, and as long as the grinding cycle is not prolonged or hurried enough to heat the mixture appreciably, there's really no difference in flavor between a pesto so produced and the pounded variety.

Specialty-food stores usually carry a variety of pestos. For the recipe given here, I used a standard basil version purchased ready-made at the supermarket. The resulting bread did not emerge from its pan green enough to mitigate my winter mood. However, it proved its worth as a hearty, compact, diffcrcnt-tasting herb bread with a mild bite nicely complementing, say, a rich vegetable soup.

> *¹/₂ cup milk, whole or skim*
> *1 egg*
> *1 tablespoon olive oil*
> *3 tablespoons basil or other pesto*
> *2 cups unbleached all-purpose flour*
> *¹/₄ to 1 teaspoon salt to taste*
> *1¹/₂ teaspoons active dry yeast*

Measure the milk into the baking pan of your bread machine and break the egg into it. Add the olive oil, pesto, flour, salt, and, last, unless otherwise directed in the instructions for your particular machine, the yeast.

Use a quick bake cycle for this loaf.

Dill Scallion Bread

W hen a friend of mine, Chi Chiu-lang, was a student in New York City, he seemed to use scallions in almost everything I saw him cook, including scrambled eggs. Bread isn't all that common in Taiwan, not being part of traditional Chinese cuisine, but on the strength of his culinary example I once decided to toss some scallions into a loaf I was putting together. Adding dill, one of my own favorite herbs, I ended up with this tall, open-textured loaf that is superb with tuna salad.

The cottage cheese found in this recipe, as in others in the book, contributes to the tenderness of the bread. Perhaps I should also alert you to the fact that it makes the loaf extra filling.

1 cup water or vegetable broth
1 egg
1 cup cottage cheese, regular or low-fat
½ cup minced fresh scallions
2 cups unbleached all-purpose flour
1 cup whole-wheat flour
1 tablespoon sugar
1 tablespoon dill seed
¼ to 1 teaspoon salt to taste
1½ teaspoons active dry yeast

Pour the water or vegetable broth into the baking pan of your bread machine, break the egg into it, and scoop in the cupful of cottage cheese and the scallions. Add the all-purpose and whole-wheat flours, the sugar, dill, salt, and, following the directions for your particular machine, the yeast.

Bake on full cycle.

Oat Groats Bread

Oat groats have been hearty breakfast fare in this country since colonial times. But they make wonderful breads as well. Boiling water is needed to soften the groats before they can be used in bread baking, however. As yet there is no cycle for such a preliminary step on the bread machines' control panels, although at least one make does double as a rice cooker. So unless your machine has a separate yeast dispenser, allow an extra fifteen minutes or so to the preparation time for this loaf, as the groat mush must be permitted to cool to lukewarm before you proceed with the recipe. If you try to throw all the ingredients in at once, the heat from the boiling water will kill the yeast.

The lecithin you'll note in the recipe is included because as a natural emulsifier it helps solid whole-grain breads to rise and hold together. The resulting loaf is hearty but not heavy.

1 cup oat groats
1½ cups boiling water
¼ cup honey
2 tablespoons olive oil
1½ cups whole-wheat flour
1 cup rye flour
2 tablespoons nonfat dry milk
1 tablespoon lecithin
1 teaspoon dried mint
½ to 1 teaspoon salt to taste
1½ teaspoons active dry yeast

Put the groats in the baking pan of your bread machine and pour the boiling water over them. If your machine features a separate dispenser for yeast, you can proceed with the recipe at this point. Otherwise you will need to wait fifteen minutes or so until the groat mixture has cooled to a lukewarm temperature before continuing. Add the honey, olive oil, whole-wheat and rye flours, dry milk, lecithin, dried mint, and salt to the batter. Scatter the yeast over the dry ingredients or add it to the yeast dispenser if your machine has one.

Bake this loaf on a regular full cycle.

7 · Savory Breads

 IT'S AMAZING what-all is stuffed into breads these days. In some cases the results go, if you'll pardon the near pun, against the grain. Blueberry bagels, for instance — nice alliteration that, but as a concept the combination just doesn't strike me right. If bagel dough is to be filled with anything, surely it should be something savory, not sweet.

The traditional savory breads are a category of the staff of life unto themselves, usually incorporating some form of meat, fish, or dairy protein to supply a more balanced diet. Simply spread with butter, their slices are like a flavorful sandwich all made up and ready to go.

Cheddar Semolina Bread

A light bread with a subtle taste of cheese, this loaf, like most cheese breads, achieves its maximum flavor when it has just cooled to room temperature after its spell in the oven. The semolina flour, normally associated with pasta, and available from health-food stores and ethnic markets, adds a nice, slightly nutty accent. The potato adds lightness and keeping quality. Whenever you cook up potatoes, incidentally, save the water they boiled in for this or another loaf.

Leftovers of this bread, if there are any, make great croutons for minestrone and other full-bodied soups. They're also excellent scattered over a spinach salad.

¾ cup plain or potato water
2 tablespoons unsalted butter or canola oil
¾ cup shredded cheddar cheese
½ cup mashed boiled potato
½ cup unbleached all-purpose flour
1½ cups semolina flour
1 tablespoon sugar
¼ to ½ teaspoon salt to taste
1½ teaspoons active dry yeast

Unless directed by the instructions for your particular bread machine to reserve the moist ingredients for adding last, pour the water into your baking pan and add the butter or canola oil, the cheddar cheese, and the mashed potato. Measure in the all-purpose and semolina flours, the sugar, and salt to taste. Add the yeast as directed for your machine.

This loaf is best baked on full cycle.

Blue Cheese Bread

Our son, Revell, has a rather exotic cheese palate for a ten-year-old, his two favorites being blue and Asiago. For years now he's been alternating Asiago with peanut butter and tuna salad sandwiches in his school lunch box. Blue cheese, however, was always a bit too crumbly to stay between the bread slices, and so did not feature in his lunch menus. Enter, I thought, my blue cheese bread.

As it turns out, this loaf, almost overwhelmingly redolent of blue cheese while baking, has a rather more subtle taste once cooled. The texture is really lovely, and though dense, the bread is not heavy. Slathered with butter, it makes an excellent appetizer to serve with beer or a hearty red wine.

1 cup milk, whole or skim
1 egg
1 tablespoon unsalted butter or canola
   oil
½ to 1 cup crumbled blue cheese to
   taste
1½ cups unbleached all-purpose flour
1 cup whole-wheat flour
2 tablespoons nonfat dry milk
1 tablespoon sugar
¼ to ½ teaspoon salt to taste
½ teaspoon white pepper
1½ teaspoons active dry yeast

   Pour the milk into your baking pan, break in the egg, and add the butter or canola oil and the blue cheese. Then measure in the all-purpose and whole-wheat flours, the dry milk, sugar, salt, pepper, and yeast. If the instructions for your machine call for putting the yeast in the pan first, follow it with the dry ingredients before adding the milk, egg, butter or oil, and cheese.

   Bake on full cycle, using a light setting, if available, for a golden, not too dark crust.

Cottage Cheese Bread

Cottage cheese adds a certain texture and moisture to bread, helping to create a tall, tender loaf that is also filling. In the recipe given here, its powers are augmented by the lecithin, which in its capacity as a natural wetting agent and emulsifier assists in the mixing of the ingredients and interacts with the gluten of the flour to increase the elasticity and rising potential of the dough.

Any cheese bread is at its most flavorsome about an hour after baking, when it has set. But this is the only loaf I know of that tastes better the next day.

1/2 cup water
1/4 cup honey
1 egg
2 tablespoons unsalted butter or canola
* oil*
3/4 cup creamy cottage cheese
2 cups unbleached all-purpose flour
1/4 cup nonfat dry milk
2 tablespoons lecithin
1/4 to 1 teaspoon salt to taste
1 1/2 teaspoons active dry yeast

Pour the water into the baking pan of your bread machine and add the honey, egg, butter or canola oil, and cottage cheese, unless the directions for your machine specify that the yeast is to be placed in the pan first, in which case you will need to reverse the order in which you add the dry and the liquid ingredients. Measure in the flour, dry milk, lecithin, salt, and yeast, following the instructions for the leavening provided with your machine.

Bake on a quick cycle.

Pepperoni Bread

More meat loaves have bread in them than bread loaves have meat. But there are a number of prepared meats, particularly sausages, that blend well into a loaf of bread. Pepperoni, with its distinctive spicy flavor, is one of them.

If you have leftover broth from cooking vegetables or potatoes in the past couple of days, this is an excellent place to dispose of it. Such a savory bread can only benefit from the extra flavor and nutrition it will add.

A favorite with the kids more than myself, our pepperoni bread inevitably ends up as thick slices in the toaster oven bearing slabs of cheese, usually cheddar and mozzarella, the latter for stretch, but often also strewn with grated Asiago or Romano for extra zest.

1 cup water or vegetable broth
2 tablespoons unsalted butter or canola
  oil
1/2 cup pepperoni, cut into 1/4-inch
  chunks
2 cups unbleached all-purpose flour
1/2 cup rye flour
1 tablespoon sugar
1 teaspoon dried oregano
1/4 to 1 teaspoon salt to taste
1 1/2 teaspoons active dry yeast

Pour the water or vegetable broth into the baking pan of your bread machine and add the butter or canola oil, pepperoni chunks, all-purpose and rye flours, sugar, oregano, and salt. Last, add the yeast, unless the instructions for your bread machine call for putting it in first, in which case the dry ingredients should be added before the water, butter or oil, and pepperoni.

This loaf does well on a quick bake cycle.

Caper Anchovy Bread

A nchovies and capers are two of those highly distinctive objects of taste that allow little room for indifference: they are approached with either relish or disgust. In our household I'm outvoted on both; no one else will touch either one of them, although the kids do eat Susan's delightful remoulade sauce with smoked fresh-caught bluefish every fall, apparently oblivious of its contents.

This bread incorporates both problematical ingredients and will presumably appeal only to anchovy and caper fanatics. Still, it's a nice moist loaf with an unusual flavor.

Note that the recipe calls for neither oil nor salt. There's plenty of both in a can of anchovies.

> *1½ cups water*
> *¼ cup capers, drained*
> *1 2-ounce can anchovies, including oil*
> *2 cups unbleached all-purpose flour*
> *1 cup rye flour*
> *½ cup cornmeal*
> *1½ teaspoons active dry yeast*

Pour the water into the baking pan of your bread machine, unless the instructions for your particular machine specify that the leavening is to be placed in the pan first and the liquids last. Add the capers, anchovies, all-purpose and rye flours, and cornmeal. Distribute the yeast according to the instructions for your machine.

Bake on full cycle.

8 · Vegetable Breads

ZUCCHINI BREAD no doubt owes its origins to the incredibly fecund nature of its vegetable component. As anyone who has grown this squash can attest, a couple of plants soon overwhelm a family's appetite unless the vegetables are consistently devoured in their most petite form — as is fashionable, for perhaps understandable reasons.

Moving the zucchini from the dinner menu to the bread basket provides welcome relief at a certain stage of summer. At the same time, zucchini has much to contribute to bread in the way of flavor and smoothness of texture. This is true of vegetables, and their cooking water, as a whole.

Almost endless variations on vegetable breads can be conceived. Those represented among the recipes in this chapter include some that readers might naturally expect to find here and some that are more startling. The aforementioned. zucchini loaf will be found among the quick-bread recipes.

Onion Soup Bread

Certain so-called prepared foods dominate contemporary cuisine, often replacing in both our memories and our loyalties the original dishes they set out to imitate. Oreo cookies come immediately to mind. So does canned tomato soup.

Perhaps none of these concoctions more typifies the culinary shortcut than dehydrated onion soup. Packets of it are dumped into everything from meat loaves to sour cream. For many people, dehydrated onion soup has become the third most-used spice after salt and pepper.

It should come as no surprise, then, that in due course I decided to try dumping a packet of dehydrated onion soup into a bread dough I was assembling. It should come as no surprise, either, that it worked very well.

Considering the convenience of bread machines, dehydrated onion soup is a natural timesaving ingredient. It also yields a very moist, tasty, nicely oniony loaf, even if the onions themselves do not remain very visible.

This loaf is highly aromatic both during baking and afterward. It's one of those breads I call real estate specials: if you're trying to sell a house, put the ingredients for this loaf into your bread machine pan and set the timer so it will finish baking just when the prospective buyer is expected to arrive. A kitchen redolent with its scent could well sell the house by itself.

A packet of dehydrated onion soup contains plenty of salt, and most people will probably find no more is needed in the recipe. But if you like a salty bread, by all means add a dash.

The soup packets themselves range in size from 1½ to 2½ ounces. Use whatever size you have handy; anything in this range works well.

1 1/4 cups buttermilk
2 tablespoons unsulphured molasses
2 tablespoons unsalted butter or canola
  oil
1 packet dehydrated onion soup
2 cups unbleached all-purpose flour
1/2 cup cornmeal
dash salt (optional)
1 1/2 teaspoons active dry yeast

Pour the buttermilk into the baking pan of your bread machine and add the molasses, butter or canola oil, onion soup mix, flour, cornmeal, and salt if desired. Distribute the yeast according to the instructions given for the particular bread machine you have.

Bake on a quick cycle.

Quick Tomato Bread

This particular loaf of bread has a full-bodied tomato taste that goes well with stews and hearty winter soups. It also has olives in it. They come under the category of optional ingredients.

Needless to say, the kids have taken to making grilled cheese sandwiches from this bread. Myself, I like to toast a thick slice, cover it with anchovy fillets, and dribble olive oil lightly over them.

"What can you expect," the rest of the family observes, "from someone who likes anchovies on pizza?"

1 cup sour cream
1 egg
1 teaspoon olive oil
1 6-ounce can tomato paste
1/2 cup pitted black olives, well drained
  (optional)

2 cups unbleached all-purpose flour
1/2 cup whole-wheat flour
1/2 cup cornmeal
1 teaspoon sugar
1 teaspoon garlic powder or 2 cloves
   fresh garlic, pressed
1 teaspoon dried basil
1 teaspoon white pepper
1/2 to 1 teaspoon salt to taste
1 1/2 teaspoons active dry yeast

Pour the sour cream into the baking pan of your bread machine, break in the egg, and add the olive oil. Scoop the tomato paste into the pan, toss in the olives if desired, and add the all-purpose and whole-wheat flours, the cornmeal, sugar, garlic, basil, white pepper, salt, and yeast, following the directions for leavening that came with your machine.

Bake on a quick cycle.

Garbanzo Bread

Garbanzos, or chick-peas, those light brown marble-sized staples of the salad bar, can also be useful in bread making. The starch of these legumes, like that of potatoes, produces a loaf lighter, softer, and better-keeping than many made from grain flours alone. The garbanzos also add a very nice nutty flavor to the bread. This recipe makes a medium-sized loaf, slices of which are delightful with vichyssoise and other cold vegetable soups in the summertime.

It is occasionally possible to buy garbanzo flour from specialty markets. But with a bread machine, it's just as easy to use the whole beans, as the machine does an excellent job of mincing them.

You can either soak dried garbanzos overnight in water — half a cup of dry garbanzos will yield a full cup of the beans after soaking — and then boil them until tender, or you can simply buy the chick-peas cooked and canned and ready to use. In either case, reserve the liquid to use in the bread as well. If there isn't enough liquid to make the full cup called for, eke it out with water.

1 cup water reserved from draining
canned garbanzos or cooking dried
ones
1 tablespoon olive oil
1 cup canned garbanzos or 1 cup
cooked garbanzos
3 cups whole-wheat flour
2 tablespoons nonfat dry milk
1 tablespoon dark brown sugar
1/2 teaspoon pepper
1/4 to 1 teaspoon salt to taste
1 1/2 teaspoons active dry yeast

Pour the garbanzo water into the baking pan of your bread machine and add the olive oil, the garbanzos themselves, then the flour, dry milk, brown sugar, pepper, and salt. Distribute the yeast according to the directions given for the particular bread machine you have.

Bake on full cycle.

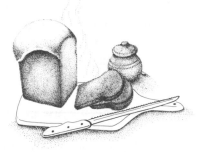

Carrot Bread

Here's a lovely saffron-colored loaf flecked with orange that makes a delightful accompaniment to a consommé or an omelet. The carrot taste is subtle, but lends a nice background flavor to this moist, sunny, high-domed bread.

My wife, Susan, upon reading this manuscript, asked why there were basil and onion in a carrot bread recipe. The answer is simple: I like basil and onions with my carrots. Since there were no leftovers when I baked this loaf, I assume the combination has general appeal. If your tastes are more traditional, you might want to substitute a teaspoon and a half of dill for the basil and onion. But then sometime do try a loaf with the basil and onion; it really is tasty.

Note that in this recipe there is relatively little liquid, only half a cup of water to two cups of flour. That's because the carrots contain a surprising amount of moisture, and a more normal measure of liquid will cause the dough to overflow the pan onto the heating element. I speak from some very messy experience here.

> *1/2 cup water*
> *1 tablespoon honey*
> *2 tablespoons unsalted butter or canola oil*
> *1 cup coarsely shredded raw carrots,*
>   *well packed*
> *2 cups unbleached all-purpose flour*
> *2 tablespoons nonfat dry milk*
> *1 teaspoon dried basil or, if preferred,*
>   *1 1/2 teaspoons dried dill*
> *1 teaspoon dehydrated minced onion*
>   *(omit if using dill)*
> *1/4 to 1/2 teaspoon salt to taste*
> *1 1/2 teaspoons active dry yeast*

Place the water, honey, and butter or canola oil in your baking pan and shake in the shredded carrots, unless the instructions for your machine specify that the liquid ingredients are to be added last and the yeast first. Next add the flour, dry milk, basil and onion, or dill if preferred, and salt. Measure in the yeast, following the instructions for the specific model of bread machine you have.

This loaf is best baked on a quick cycle with a light setting if your machine provides such a choice, as the heavier crust produced with the darker setting detracts somewhat from the delicacy of the bread.

Creamy Pumpkin Bread

In the country, the squash family turns into a cornucopia of over-abundance during the summer and fall months. Pumpkins, especially when one is trying to produce a mammoth specimen for the front porch by Halloween, as we do every year, lead to wretched excess. It's true, of course, that, properly stored, they do keep well into the wintertime. But there's only so much space one can devote to the things.

On the other hand, pumpkin is a splendid addition to bread, adding nutrition and flavor as well as moisture and texture — not that one could ever bake enough loaves to deplete significantly the likes of the 82-pound orange monster that a vine next to our barn produced last year, and certainly not with this recipe, which calls for a mere half cupful of the stuff.

Those without rampaging pumpkin vines in their gardens are spared the dilemma of disposing of excess pumpkin creatively. Pie-ready canned pumpkin works just as well in bread as pumpkin fresh from the field, cooked at home.

The absence of liquid in the recipe given here is no mistake. Pumpkins are 98 percent water, and the sour cream listed among the ingredients provides all the additional moisture needed. In fact, if you dump the sour cream and the pumpkin into your pan in one fell swoop and try to weigh them down with the other ingredients, the mixing blade, once engaged, will go round and round in the soft mush at the bottom, never drawing down the flour. To assure a proper mixing and kneading of this batter, the sour cream and pumpkin must be incorporated alternately with the dry ingredients.

1 cup sour cream
2 cups unbleached all-purpose flour
½ cup canned or freshly cooked and
   mashed pumpkin
2 tablespoons unsulphured molasses
2 tablespoons unsalted butter or canola
   oil
½ cup buckwheat flour
1 teaspoon pumpkin pie spice
¼ to 1 teaspoon salt to taste
1½ teaspoons active dry yeast

Spoon half a cupful of the sour cream into the baking pan of your bread machine, add half a cupful of the all-purpose flour, then the rest of the sour cream followed by another half cupful of flour. Next, add the pumpkin and the remaining cupful of all-purpose flour. Then measure in the molasses and butter or canola oil, the buckwheat flour, pumpkin pie spice, salt, and yeast. If your machine has a separate dispenser for leavening, the yeast should be placed there.

Bake on a quick cycle.

9 · Sweet Breads

 THE BOUNDARY BETWEEN cakes and coffee breads is not a well marked frontier. Cakes are usually moister and lighter — but not always. Certainly a good *Pischinger* or *Sachertorte* could not be described as light. Both do have icings, of course, whereas breads don't. Then again, a dark, rich molasses glaze studded with slivered almonds is almost as sweet, and certainly as striking, as a cake frosting.

But why worry about semantics? If there's any doubt in your mind that a good coffee bread can satisfy the most imperious of sweet cravings, just let the taste buds loose on a mouthful of two-chocolates bread. You'll forget all about mundane distinctions.

The recipes in this chapter all list yeast as their leavener. Many baking-powder breads are scrumptiously sweet as well, however. They're in another spot simply because their manner of construction, so to speak, is different.

Sally Lunn

Sally Lunn is a familiar listing in the repertory of the home bakery. Butter-rich and golden from the egg yolks in it, this sweet bread is one that could easily slip unnoticed over the border into the realm of cakes.

Its name, like that of Anadama bread, has different legendary sources. It is often attributed to the French *soleil et lune,* or sun and moon, the association deriving presumably from the golden crust and white underside of the buns into which the dough was traditionally shaped. In another story, it is the namesake of an English villager who peddled her homemade cakes on the streets of Bath; a local baker was so taken with the buns that he began to bake them himself, but sold them as Sally Lunn's.

> *3/4 cup milk, whole or skim*
> *2 eggs*
> *6 tablespoons unsalted butter*
> *2 cups unbleached all-purpose flour*
> *1/4 cup sugar*
> *1/4 to 1 teaspoon salt to taste*
> *2 teaspoons active dry yeast*

Pour the milk into your bread machine's baking pan and break the eggs into it, unless the instructions that came with your machine call for placing the yeast in the bottom of the pan and reserving the liquids till last, adding them after the dry ingredients. Since you're using a fair amount of butter, cut it into chunks if it's hard, so it will blend into the dough more uniformly, before adding it to the liquid ingredients. Then measure in the flour, sugar, salt, and yeast.

This attractive high loaf can be baked on your machine's quick cycle.

Raisin Bread

There was one whole week shortly after first bringing home a bread machine during which I baked nothing but raisin bread, sometimes two or three loaves a day. This was not because we are inordinately fond of raisin bread, but because I was striving for a loaf with whole raisins in it.

The batter blade at the bottom of a bread machine pan stirs and kneads the dough rather fiercely. This hyperactivity is a technological compromise between applying enough motion to the dough to render it elastic and pliant and keeping the size of the blade small enough so that the baked loaf is not torn asunder when pulled out of the pan.

Unfortunately, the violent motion shreds chunky ingredients like raisins to puny pieces in the machine's regular cycle, which is the one it utilizes automatically unless instructed otherwise. I tried everything I could think of to keep the raisins whole, from freezing them beforehand to candying them. Nothing worked.

But why, you might ask, if it's only in the regular cycle that the raisins are mashed, didn't I simply bake the bread on the quick cycle?

Good question. The fact is that if you bake raisin bread on a quick cycle, as the instruction manual tells you to do, you will get bread with whole raisins. *However, you cannot use the quick cycle and the timer together, and if you want freshly baked bread in the morning, you have to use the timer.* My problem was that I think of raisin bread as something one eats in the morning, and wanted it for breakfast.

That still unsolved conundrum aside, the recipe given here makes a very tasty raisin bread — with plenty of whole raisins, clearly visible and bursting with flavor.

1 cup milk, whole or skim
1 tablespoon unsalted butter or canola
*   oil*

1 cup raisins
2 cups unbleached all-purpose flour
2 tablespoons dark brown sugar
1½ teaspoons cinnamon
¼ to 1 teaspoon salt to taste
2 teaspoons active dry yeast

Pour the milk into the baking pan of your bread machine and add the spoonful of butter or canola oil and the raisins, unless your machine has a mix cycle permitting you to add the raisins separately, for greater fullness, after the other ingredients have been blended. Measure in the flour, brown sugar, cinnamon, salt, and yeast. For placement of the yeast, follow the directions provided with your bread machine.

Bake this loaf on a quick cycle.

Maple Oat Bread

To our good fortune, a neighbor, Chappie Rich, besides running an efficient dairy farm, graces country living for local residents and wayfarers alike with newly pressed cider from his mill, fresh fruits and vegetables, and, in early spring, rich maple syrup from his busy sugarhouse. He taps our sugar bush, as maple groves are known, and gives us gallons of beautiful syrup in return. Hence this somewhat extravagant recipe.

The loaf that results, retaining a lingering flavor of maple, is devoured with much delight by our children, who dieters would with some justification maintain add insult to injury by slathering it with maple butter! Substituting maple-flavored syrup for the real thing in the recipe not only works, but probably makes more sense if one isn't fortunate enough to have a sugar bush out back and someone nearby offering to tap it.

¾ cup water
½ cup maple or maple-flavored syrup
2 tablespoons unsalted butter or canola
oil
2½ cups unbleached all-purpose flour
1 cup uncooked oatmeal (not instant)
¼ to 1 teaspoon salt to taste
1½ teaspoons active dry yeast

Pour the water and the maple syrup into the baking pan of your bread machine, add the butter or canola oil, then measure in the flour, oatmeal, salt, and yeast, unless directed by the instructions for your particular machine to place the yeast in the pan first, in which case the dry ingredients should be added before the liquids.

Set your machine to its full cycle for this loaf.

Spiced Raisin Pumpernickel Bread

True pumpernickel is traditionally a sourdough bread, coarse-grained and dark, made from unsifted rye flour. Its Eulenspiegel-esque name derives from the combination of two German words: *pumpern,* to break wind — the idea being that the coarse bread was very difficult to digest — and *Nickel,* a goblin or demon — whose friendlier side is represented by jolly old Saint Nick.

The recipe offered here results in a much milder pumpernickel than that which presumably first earned the name. The loaf is high-domed, with a very soft, silky texture.

The cocoa is included more for the traditional dark color of rye breads than for anything else. The raisins are optional. Revell, raisined out on school-lunch-box-sized cartons of them, prefers the bread without. But if you omit the raisins, you may need to reduce the yeast by half a teaspoon to keep the bread from topping out in your machine.

1 1/2 cups water
1/4 cup unsulphured molasses
1/4 cup unsalted butter or canola oil
1 cup raisins (optional)
2 cups unbleached all-purpose flour
1 cup rye flour
1 cup whole-wheat flour
1/4 cup cocoa
1 tablespoon cinnamon
1/4 to 1 teaspoon salt to taste
2 teaspoons active dry yeast (or 1 1/2
  teaspoons if the raisins are omitted)

Pour the water and molasses into your bread machine's baking pan and add the butter, cut into small chunks if it's not soft, to ensure that it blends uniformly into the dough, or substitute canola oil, if you prefer. Next add the raisins, if desired, and the all-purpose, rye, and whole-wheat flours. Measure in the cocoa, cinnamon, and salt. Distribute the yeast according to the directions for your particular machine, remembering to reverse the order in which you add the liquid and the dry ingredients if the instructions for your machine specify that the yeast be placed at the bottom of the pan.

Set your machine on its quick cycle for this loaf.

Almond Bread

We don't have a strawberry patch. We do have enough blue-berry bushes to reap a bountiful harvest from them every year; our daughters, Genevieve and Tanya, used to sell the surplus from a roadside buckboard to earn extra preteen summer spending money. We also have currants and gooseberries galore, not to mention a wild bramble patch supplying an abundance of succulent raspberries and blackberries. Every spring I announce that this is the year when we're going to put in a strawberry patch, and every year we end up heading for a pick-your-own berry farm instead. There's just too much to be done around the place, I guess.

But when we head for the berry farm to pick strawberries, I toss all the ingredients for this almond loaf into the bread machine before we go and set the timer for our return. The bread has a heavenly fragrance of marzipan and a rich almond taste, and a generous square of it served warm in a bowl heaped high with strawberries and cov-ered with cream makes a superlative shortcake. For extra verve use a dark corn syrup glaze and sprinkle with slivered almonds.

1 cup milk, whole or skim
1 egg
3 tablespoons unsalted butter
1 8-ounce can almond paste, cut into
*   about 1/8-inch slices for better blending*
2 1/2 cups unbleached all-purpose flour
2 tablespoons dark brown sugar
1/4 to 1/2 teaspoon salt to taste
2 teaspoons active dry yeast

GLAZE
1 teaspoon dark corn syrup
1 teaspoon warm water
slivered almonds for garnish

Unless the instructions that came with your machine call for putting the yeast in the pan first and incorporating the liquid ingredients last, pour the milk into the baking pan of your bread machine and break in the egg. If the butter is not soft, cut it into small chunks to ensure its blending into the dough, then add it to the liquids. Next add the almond paste, sliced so it will blend better too. Measure in the flour, brown sugar, and salt, and add the yeast as directed for your bread maker.

You can use your machine's full cycle with this bread, but the quick cycle is better. If a light color setting is available, use it as well. As soon as the bread has finished baking, remove it from the machine, closing the cover again, and ease the loaf from its pan. Combine the corn syrup and warm water and brush the top of the loaf with this mixture, using a pastry brush. Sprinkle the slivered almonds over the glaze, put the bread gently back in its pan, and return it to the electronic oven for a few minutes to dry the glaze a bit.

Bread of Two Chocolates

B read and chocolate have been a popular combination in Europe for a long time. A rather good little Swiss movie called *Bread and Chocolate* even took its name from their amiable fraternization a while back.

The coalition originated, I suspect, as a handy lunch among hikers. I remember being sustained on many wanderings in my youth by a couple of strips of *Landjäger,* that hard, dry German sausage that will last without refrigeration seemingly considerably longer than the teeth that chew it, a hearty hunk of rye bread, and a chocolate bar for extra energy.

The chocolate on those occasions was usually the bittersweet kind, and I inevitably ended up alternating bites of it with chunks of the firm, rough-textured bread. They went wonderfully together. I guess that, in essence, is how otherwise strange but good combinations are discovered.

This particular loaf is soft and moist. Its fine texture, due in part to the use of semolina flour, is riddled with distinct bits of tasty chocolate. The loaf is not truly sweet, and it's certainly not a cake. But try it with Nutella if you can find that concoction. This chocolate hazelnut spread from France is much loved by our children, who discovered it during a family sojourn in the village of Restinclières in the south of France. They found it quite irresistible spooned lavishly onto chunks of crisp-crusted French bread fresh from the bakery down the lane.

Lacking Nutella, try the bread with peppermint butter. The mint contributes a totally unexpected sparkle that beautifully complements tea.

> *1 cup milk, whole or skim*
> *2 tablespoons unsalted butter*
> *1 teaspoon vanilla extract*
> *¾ cup semisweet chocolate chips*
> *½ cup walnuts, coarsely chopped*
> *1½ cups unbleached all-purpose flour*
> *1 cup semolina flour*
> *⅓ cup nonfat dry milk*
> *3 tablespoons sugar*
> *2 tablespoons cocoa·*
> *1 tablespoon instant espresso*
> *¼ to 1 teaspoon salt to taste*
> *½ teaspoon baking soda*
> *1½ teaspoons yeast*

Remember that if the instructions that came with your bread machine call for the leavening to be placed in the baking pan first, the other dry ingredients should be added next, before the liquid ingredients. Otherwise, pour the milk into the pan and measure in the butter, vanilla extract, chocolate chips, and walnuts. Add the all-purpose and semolina flours, the dry milk, sugar, cocoa, instant espresso, salt, baking soda, and, if the instructions for your machine so direct, the yeast. If your machine has a separate dispenser for leavening, spoon the yeast into the dispenser after all the other ingredients have been measured into the baking pan.

Use a quick bake cycle for this loaf.

PEPPERMINT BUTTER

½ cup unsalted butter, softened
1 tablespoon confectioners' sugar
½ teaspoon peppermint extract

Cream the butter and powdered sugar until smooth. Add the peppermint extract and blend well. Serve with a sprig of fresh mint from the garden.

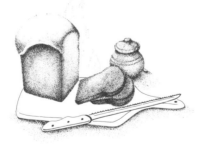

10 · Ethnic Breads

FOR BAKING INSPIRATION, the traditional loaves of Europe are hard to beat. Quite literally, they come in a thousand varieties. Bread has been the staff of life for millennia and is so central to daily life on the Continent that in Germany a whole museum is dedicated to the commodity.

Bread, in all its ethnic variety, has also served as a daily reminder of the old country to immigrants in America, who have kept their local baking traditions alive long after their other customs have faded into obscurity. Wander through any ethnic neighborhood and you will find there a bakery turning out loaf after loaf of some treasured bread from the homeland, be it Lithuanian rye, Swedish saffron bread, Norwegian *lefse,* or a dark German pumpernickel. I've baked cardamom bread for decades from an old family recipe brought over from Sweden. The recipe as adapted for the bread machine makes a delicious loaf, albeit not one plaited in the traditional manner.

Scandinavian Limpa

L impa is a Scandinavian rye bread redolent of anise or fennel, caraway, and orange. The exact combination and proportions of the flavorings vary from country to country and even from town to town. There are also fancy versions of the bread for the Christmas holidays.

The taste of a thick slice of limpa spread with butter and *messmör,* a soft sweet Swedish goat cheese, will always be one of my fondest childhood memories. *Messmör* has the consistency of peanut butter and, in fact, is Sweden's popular equivalent of that all-American spread. It is hardly ever available in the States, but many specialty cheese stores carry a Norwegian hard version called *gjetost.* If you grate this cheese and beat it with heavy cream to a smooth consistency, you come close to the *messmör* of my childhood.

In like fashion, the recipe given here approximates the limpa I remember, though it's not the same. I'd blame this on the bread machine were it not for the fact that I've never been able to duplicate that now distant loaf by traditional methods either. Maybe you just can't bake home again.

1½ cups milk, whole or skim
2 tablespoons canola oil
2 tablespoons unsulphured molasses
2 cups unbleached all-purpose flour
1 cup rye flour
2 tablespoons dark brown sugar
1 tablespoon cocoa
1 tablespoon grated orange rind
1 teaspoon aniseed, lightly crushed
½ teaspoon caraway seeds
¼ to 1 teaspoon salt to taste
1½ teaspoons active dry yeast

Pour the milk into the baking pan of your bread machine and measure in first the oil, then the molasses, unless the instructions for your machine specify that the yeast is to be put in the bottom of the pan, followed by the other dry and then the liquid ingredients. Add the all-purpose and rye flours, the brown sugar, cocoa, orange rind, aniseed, caraway seeds, and salt. Distribute the yeast as directed for your machine.

Bake on a quick cycle.

Russian Black Bread

Here's one of my favorite breads. Still not as black as some of the loaves of European rye my memory conjures up, even with both cocoa and coffee added for color, it's nevertheless very dark and moist and dense.

For all that, it's fairly light in heft. One of the secrets here is the use of bread crumbs in the recipe. Such a reclamation of crumbs may seem the ultimate in modern recycling to bread machine owners with leftover loaves, but it's an age-old custom serving a much more basic function. Bread crumbs add airiness, whether to bread or dumplings or a torte.

You can use either store-bought crumbs, for convenience, or your own homemade variety (see the instructions on making bread crumbs in the chapter "After the Loaf"). Toasting the crumbs is really worth the small effort involved. They can be browned either in the oven or in a skillet over a burner.

For oven toasting, spread the crumbs out on a cookie sheet and pop them into a preheated 400-degree oven for eight to ten minutes or until they are a deep golden brown. For stovetop toasting, which I prefer because it's quicker, put the crumbs in an ungreased steel fry pan over a medium to high flame. Stir continuously until the crumbs are the color of dark oak.

The bread crumbs in this recipe help to lighten the loaf, which would otherwise have the solidness characteristic of so many rye breads. You might note that in the list of ingredients the rye and whole-wheat flours appear first, before the liquids usually heading the roster. This reversal is to improve the mixing, which otherwise is poor because of the large quantity of liquid this recipe calls for.

A good Russian black bread really deserves a befitting glaze. The standard one would be simply egg and water. But a mustard glaze goes very well with this loaf, and sesame seeds on top of that add a superlative burst of flavor.

The bread keeps well, although in our family it's rarely allowed to do so because of its popularity. Great slabs of it with generous slices of meat and a favorite condiment between them make wonderful hearty sandwiches. Try it thinly sliced for canapés as well; it's an excellent foil, both in flavor and in appearance, for savory spreads.

> *1 cup rye flour*
> *1/2 cup whole-wheat flour*
> *2 cups warm water*
> *2 tablespoons instant espresso*
> *2 tablespoons unsulphured molasses*
> *2 tablespoons unsalted butter or canola oil*
> *1 1/2 cups unbleached all-purpose flour*
> *1 cup toasted bread crumbs*
> *1 tablespoon cocoa*
> *2 teaspoons aniseed*
> *1 1/2 teaspoons caraway seeds*
> *1/4 to 1 teaspoon salt to taste*
> *1 1/2 teaspoons active dry yeast*
>
> *GLAZE*
> *1 egg*
> *1 tablespoon prepared whole-grain mustard*
> *sesame seeds for garnish*

Measure the rye and whole-wheat flours into the baking pan of your bread machine. Pour the water into a separate bowl or a large measuring cup and dissolve the instant espresso in it. Then transfer the dilute coffee to the baking pan, add the molasses, butter or canola oil, all-purpose flour, bread crumbs, cocoa, aniseed, caraway seeds, salt, and yeast. If your machine has a separate dispenser for leavening, the yeast should be placed there.

A full bake cycle is needed for this bread, to give the dough time to rise properly. As soon as the bread is baked, remove it from its pan. Whip the egg and mustard together and brush this mixture onto the hot loaf with a pastry brush. Sprinkle with sesame seeds if desired. Slip the loaf back into its pan and return it to the bread machine, where the residual heat will bake the glaze on.

Hungarian Potato Bread

Potato bread began as an adulteration. Clean, pure wheat flour remained for centuries both expensive and hard to come by. Accordingly, millers and tradesmen used everything from talcum powder to ground bleached bones to stretch their salable supply of flour.

It's not surprising, then, that when the potato made its way to European shores, a mealed version of it was forthwith utilized to help eke out the merchants' stores of flour. What did come as a surprise was the way in which the addition of potato to the wheat flour actually improved the baked goods resulting from the mix.

In a family of five such as ours, as often as not there's a leftover potato or two to be found hiding in the refrigerator. Here's a great use for such strays. If none are to be found on the day you decide to bake this loaf and you boil up a potato just for the bread, by all means save the water in which the potato cooks to use in the dough as well.

Soft, light, and very open-textured, this bread makes superlative toast. It also makes a delightful sandwich with ham or salami -- Hungarian, naturally — tucked between its slices and crisp sour pickles on the side. If the caraway seeds are omitted from the recipe, the loaf, sliced thick, makes wonderful French toast.

>*1 cup potato or plain water*
>*½ cup mashed boiled potato*
>*2 cups unbleached all-purpose flour*
>*1 tablespoon sugar*
>*2 teaspoons caraway seeds (optional)*
>*¼ to 1 teaspoon salt to taste*
>*1½ teaspoons active dry yeast*

Pour the potato water or, lacking that, plain water into the baking pan of your bread machine and add the mashed potato, flour, sugar, caraway seeds if desired, salt, and yeast, following the directions for leavening that came with your particular machine.

Use a quick bake cycle for this loaf.

French Walnut Bread

As taste and texture go, walnuts have a rather soft crunch, and in a bread machine, the kneading blade chops the pieces for you, so don't hesitate to use whole halves. The recipe given here produces a dense, nut-brown loaf with a fine, pebbly texture. The bread is rich and earthy and goes well with Neufchâtel and other soft cheeses.

>*½ cup milk, whole or skim*
>*1 egg*
>*4 tablespoons walnut oil*
>*1½ cups walnut halves or large pieces*
>*2 cups unbleached all-purpose flour*
>*1 teaspoon sugar*
>*¼ to 1 teaspoon salt to taste*
>*1½ teaspoons active dry yeast*

Unless the instructions that came with your machine specify that the yeast is to be placed in your baking pan first, followed by the dry and then the liquid ingredients, pour the milk into the pan and break the egg into it. Add the walnut oil and the walnuts, then the flour, sugar, salt, and yeast.

Use a quick bake cycle for this loaf.

Scandinavian Cardamom Bread

A cardamom braid is my favorite coffee bread, although saffron bread is a close second on my list. I bake four long plaited cardamom loaves almost every Saturday morning during the fall and winter. By Monday after school they're usually gone — and I've not consumed more than half a dozen slices myself. Honest.

No machine-baked bread will ever replace the long golden-brown braids glistening with pearl sugar that I have associated with cardamom bread since my childhood. The aesthetic ingraining of those early years simply won't allow such a trade-in. However, with the recipe given here it is possible to capture, if not the original visual appeal, then at least the flavor and fragrance of true cardamom bread. Besides, the loaf is a handsome one even in its more modern form, its golden dome studded with pearl sugar.

Although not readily available in most local grocery shops and supermarkets, pearl sugar may be purchased through some of the catalog concerns listed in the back of this book. Granulated sugar can be substituted for it in the glaze, but it's really not the same. Pearl sugar crystals are fairly large, as their name implies, and they don't dissolve into a glaze as regular sugar does, but rather remain brilliantly white and sparkling on top of a loaf.

If possible, buy whole cardamom for your baking. This will mean peeling and grinding the seed. But the flavor of freshly ground cardamom is far more intense than the pre-ground variety, which almost always includes the flavorless paperlike husk.

> *½ cup light cream*
> *1 egg*
> *¼ cup unsalted butter*
> *2½ cups unbleached all-purpose flour*
> *¼ cup sugar*
> *1 teaspoon hulled cardamom seeds,*
>   *finely ground*
> *dash salt*
> *1¼ teaspoons active dry yeast*

> *GLAZE*
> *1 egg*
> *1 tablespoon cold water*
> *pearl sugar for garnish*

Pour the cream into your bread machine pan and break the egg into it. Add the butter, cutting it into chunks first if it's hard, so it will blend more uniformly into the dough. Measure in the flour, sugar, cardamom, salt, and, following the instructions given for leavening for your particular machine, the yeast.

Use the short cycle, and a light loaf setting, if available on your machine, for best results in baking this bread. As soon as the loaf is done, pull the pan from the machine and immediately close the lid to retain heat. Remove the loaf from its pan. Beat together the egg and water and paint the top of the loaf liberally with this mixture, using a pastry brush. Sprinkle generously with pearl sugar and gently fit the bread back into its baking container. Pop the pan back into the bread machine for another two minutes or so. The residual heat of the machine will bake the glaze on, causing most of the pearl sugar to adhere. Remove the loaf to its cooling rack with care.

Swedish Saffron Bread

Saffron bread is even richer and somewhat sweeter than carda-mom bread. The trick to achieving a truly saffrony loaf, both colorwise and flavorwise, is to crumble the saffron strands or, better yet, grind them with a mortar and pestle, and steep them in very hot water in a small glass or stainless steel container for ten minutes before adding the infusion to the other ingredients.

½ cup heavy cream
2 eggs
¼ cup unsalted butter
½ teaspoon saffron strands, crumbled
    or finely ground, infused in 1 tablespoon
    hot water
2½ cups unbleached all-purpose flour
½ cup sugar
dash salt
1¼ teaspoons active dry yeast

GLAZE
    1 egg
    1 tablespoon cold water

To save time, make the saffron infusion first thing, so it can be steeping while you assemble the other ingredients. Then pour the cream into your bread machine pan and break the eggs into it. Since you are using a fair amount of butter, if it's not soft, cut it into chunks so that it will blend better into the dough, then add it to the liquids. When the saffron has steeped for ten minutes, pour the infusion into the pan and measure in the flour, sugar, salt, and, following the instructions for the leavening provided for your par-ticular machine, the yeast.

Use your machine's short cycle, and a light loaf setting if available, for this bread. As soon as it has finished baking, take the pan from the machine, closing the lid of the machine again to retain heat. Remove the loaf from its pan. Beat together the egg and water and with a pastry brush paint the top of the loaf with the glazing mixture. Then put the loaf back in its pan and return it to the bread machine for two minutes or so. The oven's residual heat will bake the glaze on.

Mock Brioche

Classic brioche, with its fluted sides and little topknot and silky texture, is, like real French bread, found only rarely outside of France. Certainly a bread machine pan cannot create the distinctive flutes or the cocky topknot, nor does the kneading blade seem capable of producing the smooth grain of true brioche. I suspect that, for all its beating and crashing the dough about, a baking machine is no match for the experienced hands of a French pastry chef. All the same, the recipe given here results in a very handsome loaf, rich in butter and eggs, with a high, rounded dome.

> *¹/₄ cup milk, whole or skim*
> *3 eggs*
> *10 tablespoons unsalted butter*
> *2¹/₂ cups unbleached all-purpose flour*
> *2 tablespoons sugar*
> *¹/₂ to 1 teaspoon salt to taste*
> *1¹/₂ teaspoons active dry yeast*

Unless the instructions that came with your machine call for placing the yeast in your bread machine pan first and reversing the order in which the liquid and other dry ingredients are incorporated into the batter, pour the milk into your baking pan and break in the eggs. Since you are using a sizable quantity of butter, if it's not soft, cut it into chunks so it will blend more easily with the other ingredients, then add it to the pan. Measure in the flour, sugar, salt, and yeast, placing the leavening in its own receptacle if your machine has one.

Use a quick bake cycle for this bread.

11 · Sourdough Breads

SOURDOUGH IS ASSOCIATED in many people's minds with cowboys and the wild West or gold panning in Alaska, but it's far older than that. Archaeologists have uncovered evidence of sourdough baking in ancient Egypt some six thousand years ago.

A sourdough culture can be started simply by capturing some rogue yeast from the wild. That's easy enough. All you have to do is to put a starchy liquid out to sour, or ferment. It can be potato water, corn mash, even leftover spaghetti in its cooking water. Whatever you use as bait, you'll catch something.

But there's a snag to this seemingly innocent endeavor. Wild yeasts do add flavor to a sourdough — sometimes a very strange flavor. And you never know until you've used the starter what that flavor is going to be like. I've encountered some dillies; one native yeast I garnered turned the inside of a bread loaf into a sodden stringy mess.

This is in no way meant to discourage you from making your own sourdough starter. You could well end up with a culture yummy enough to become an heirloom, passed on for generations as sourdough was in the days of yore. But I'd advise at least bringing the operation in from the wilds and taming it a bit.

The simplest approach to starting a sourdough indoors is to set out, in a warm spot, a glass or stainless steel bowl into which you've poured a cup of milk with a cupful of unbleached all-purpose flour and a teaspoonful of sugar beaten into it. The back of the stove or an oven warmed by a pilot light will serve admirably as a resting place for this concoction.

After some twenty-four to thirty-eight hours, your starter should have begun to foam a bit. It should also have acquired a reasonably strong sour smell. Let it stand undisturbed until the bubbles froth up, which will probably take several days. Then refrigerate the sour, as it's often called, until needed.

If the sourdough turns pink at some point in its fermentation, you have a slime culture. Throw it out and start over.

A less chancy technique is to heat a cupful of milk to wrist temperature, beat in a cupful of unbleached all-purpose flour, and add a couple of tablespoonfuls of yogurt to seed the mixture. Cover the batter tightly with plastic wrap to keep wild yeasts out. Within a few days you should have a nice bubbly sour.

The least problematical course of all is to pick up a packet of dry granular sourdough starter at a health-food store or get it by mail order — or from a tourist trap in San Francisco — and follow the accompanying instructions.

Whichever method you use, once you have a satisfactory sour, there are two keys to continued success with it. First, the starter needs to be at room temperature before use. It wouldn't hurt to take it out of the refrigerator the night before you plan to bake a sourdough loaf. Second, the started mother lode needs to be replenished every time you draw on it. Add equal parts warm milk and unbleached all-purpose flour, beaten together, equivalent in volume to the amount of starter removed for baking.

Real, honest-to-goodness sourdough bread uses no yeast in the traditional sense. The sour itself, after all, is a yeast. But when using a bread machine, a little extra leavening may be helpful, since some sours are not potent enough to leaven a batch of dough within the somewhat condensed and artificially timed period allotted by the machine for bread making.

On the other hand, some sours will produce magnificent loaves, at least of white if not the heavier whole-wheat and rye breads, all on their own. The only way to find out what your starter can and cannot do is to try it with and without — or perhaps I should say without and with — yeast.

Incidentally, timed overnight baking is probably not to be recommended for sourdough breads. While the extra hours of rest would certainly give the sour a longer interval in which to leaven the dough, there's always the possibility that it might levitate the bread right out of the pan while you slept.

You'll notice that the order in which the ingredients for the sourdough breads are listed is different from that of most of the other recipes in this book. The reason for the change in sequence is the problem of cavitation, discussed in the chapter called "Tips and Tricks for Electronic Baking."

White Sourdough Bread

The most familiar sourdough breads this side of the Atlantic are the long baguettes and Italian loaves made famous by San Franciscans. The recipe given here uses yeast as well as sourdough for leavening. While that's definitely cheating a bit, it lends to the formula a reliability that a yeastless version simply could not supply.

Using yeast to help loft the loaf also mediates the tartness of the sourdough, resulting in a bread with just a pleasant hint of sour.

Myself, I prefer my sourdough bread truly sour. If you do too, let me recommend the all-sourdough recipe. It's very sour.

Whichever recipe you choose, don't expect from your bread machine the kind of crust that shatters at the touch of the knife the way that of an old-time hearthstone-baked loaf does. The crust of this bread, though good, will not have the same remarkable crispness.

1¾ cups unbleached all-purpose flour
2 cups sourdough starter, at room temperature
1 tablespoon honey
2 tablespoons unsalted butter or canola oil
¼ to 1 teaspoon salt to taste
1 teaspoon active dry yeast

Measure the flour into the baking pan of your bread machine first, then add the sourdough starter, honey, butter or canola oil, salt, and yeast. If your model has a separate dispenser for the yeast, spoon it in there.

You can use a quick cycle for this loaf, since the sour and the yeast should, between the two of them, raise the dough on that shorter cycle with no difficulty.

Sourdough Whole-Wheat Bread

Sourdough whole-wheat bread is heartier than its white counter-part, yet not as dense as a sourdough rye. The recipe given here yields a fine sandwich loaf. Leftovers, if there are any, make choice bread crumbs for casserole toppings.

3 cups whole-wheat flour
1½ cups sourdough starter, at room temperature
½ cup warm water
2 tablespoons olive oil
¼ to 1 teaspoon salt to taste
1 teaspoon active dry yeast

Measure the flour into the baking pan for your bread machine, then pour in the starter and water and add the olive oil and salt.

Distribute the yeast according to the instructions provided with your machine.

This loaf can be baked on a quick cycle, since it does not rely on the sourdough alone for leavening power.

Sourdough Rye Bread

This comes close to the real thing in the old European tradition. The sours in Europe were always based on rye flour, which has a tendency really to ferment. However, to keep your starter from getting out of hand, I would recommend replenishing it with milk and unbleached all-purpose flour even if you regularly use it for making rye bread. A sour based on fermented rye flour tends to be too strong for all but the most fanatical devotees.

1½ cups rye flour
1½ cups whole-wheat flour
1½ cups sourdough starter, at room
*   temperature*
½ cup warm water
1 tablespoon olive oil
2 tablespoons unsulphured molasses
1 cup unbleached all-purpose flour
2 tablespoons instant espresso
1 tablespoon caraway seeds
1 tablespoon dehydrated minced onion
*   (optional)*
¼ to 1 teaspoon salt to taste
1 to 1½ teaspoons active dry yeast

Measure the rye and whole-wheat flours into the baking pan of your bread machine first, then add the sourdough starter, water, oil, and molasses, followed by the all-purpose flour, espresso, caraway seeds, onion if desired, salt, and yeast, placing the yeast in its own dispenser if your machine has such.

Use a full bake cycle for this bread. Even with the addition of yeast, the heavy flours called for make it a slow-rising loaf.

Sourdough Buckwheat Bread

Buckwheat flour, like cornmeal, is quintessentially American. Unlike corn, however, buckwheat is not native to these shores. Its cultivated origins lie somewhere in what is now China, and it has been grown in Europe, where it is served hulled and cooked in the form of kasha, for hundreds of years. Even so, as a flour it has never achieved the popularity on the Continent or in the Far East that it acquired in the States, where during the 1700s and 1800s it was a kitchen staple, particularly for making the buckwheat cakes immortalized in the song "Oh, Susannah."

The recipe given here makes a pleasant loaf of bread — if you like the earthy taste of buckwheat. Personally, I can take it or leave it. But I do have to admit that there's something especially warming about a buckwheat loaf served with a hearty stew on a cold winter's day. Maybe that's why buckwheat is so popular in Siberia.

> *1 cup unbleached all-purpose flour*
> *2 cups buckwheat flour*
> *2 cups sourdough starter, at room temperature*
> *2 tablespoons olive oil*
> *2 tablespoons honey*
> *¹/₂ to 1 teaspoon salt to taste*
> *1 teaspoon active dry yeast*

Place the all-purpose and buckwheat flours in the baking pan of your bread machine first thing, then measure in the sourdough starter, and on top of that the oil, honey, and salt. Add the yeast, placing it in the yeast dispenser if your machine has one.

Use a quick bake cycle for this loaf.

All-Sour Sourdough Bread

Here's a loaf that depends completely on its sour for leavening. Its success will stand and fall with the strength of the particular sourdough starter you have bubbling.

To help ensure a happy outcome, first of all, your starter should have the consistency of a tender pancake batter, the kind achieved from using one part flour to one part milk. If you consistently replenish your starter in those proportions, it should remain consistently dependable.

The second key to successful baking with sourdough as your sole leavening agent is to make sure that the sour has been standing unrefrigerated and bubbling, preferably in an oven with a pilot light, for at least twelve hours before being incorporated into the dough it is intended to leaven.

Third, remember to set your bread machine on its full cycle, the one that takes roughly four hours from start to finish, when using sourdough alone for leavening power. A short cycle won't allow enough time for the sour to work its magic; an overnight cycle will almost guarantee your waking to the sound of your smoke alarm and spending the morning chipping burned dough out of your bread machine.

While the recipe given here should work with most sours, you may need to add or withhold half a cupful of the measure of sour indicated, to make your bread rise more or less, respectively. Be prepared for the occasional mishap of a too heavy or an overflowing dough, for sourdough starter can be as unpredictable as a teenager.

This bread is a perfect foil for sliced salmon, tuna, sardines, and other seafood. Toasted, it invites a tangy, coarse-cut orange marmalade.

2 cups unbleached all-purpose flour
2 cups sourdough starter, at room tem-
*   perature or warmer*
2 teaspoons honey
2 tablespoons canola oil
¼ to 1 teaspoon salt to taste

Place the flour in the baking pan of your bread machine first, then add the sourdough starter, honey, oil, and salt.

Remember to set your machine on full cycle for this bread.

12 · Quick Breads

 THE BREAD MACHINES were designed to bake yeast breads. But baking powder is another useful leavening agent, and the breads raised with it are quite different in many ways from their yeast-raised cousins.

To make something like Irish soda bread or a quick bran loaf by using baking powder but adding yeast for additional leavening, as the instructions included with the bread machines suggest, really isn't cricket. It's a matter not so much of principle as of taste. I love a yeasty loaf, but not if I'm eating soda bread.

It is quite possible to make a baking-powder bread in the electronic oven if the recipe is properly adapted. However, try as I might, I've never had a real baking-soda-only bread work in the machine.

Breakfast Bran Bread

This is the loaf version of the classic bran muffin. A low loaf, it's crumbly and soft, so cut it in slabs rather than thin slices.

> 2/3 cup milk, whole or skim
> 1/2 cup unsulphured molasses
> 1 egg
> 1/4 cup solid vegetable shortening
> 1 cup unbleached all-purpose flour

1 cup unprocessed wheat bran
¼ cup firmly packed dark brown sugar
dash salt
1 tablespoon double-acting baking
*   powder*

Measure the milk and molasses into your bread pan, break in the egg, and add the shortening. Then toss in the flour, wheat bran, brown sugar, salt, and baking powder.

This baking-powder bread is best baked on a quick cycle.

Mock Boston Brown Bread

I've always liked steamed Boston brown bread. All the good fresh coffee beans that have become available in the last decade have been a boon to coffee aficionados, but not to the baked-beans-and-Boston-brown-bread set: I find we no longer have a reliable supply of coffee cans in which to steam breads and puddings.

I've called this bread a mock Boston brown bread because to my mind real Boston brown bread can be achieved only through hours of steaming in a coffee tin old enough to be just beginning to rust at the seams. All the same, this version adapted for bread machine baking, if not as moist and puddingy as the real thing, is still very tasty, and, due to the characteristic shape of bread machine pans, it's, well, almost round.

I've made this loaf with buttermilk. But running out of that commodity one day, I substituted sour cream diluted with water. The results were rewarding enough that I've stayed with the sour cream version ever since. The recipe works equally well without the raisins, a note I add for those oversaturated with plumped raisins in fruitcakes and other confections in their youth.

1 cup sour cream
1/2 cup water
1/2 cup unsulphured molasses
1 egg
1 cup raisins (optional)
1 cup unbleached all-purpose flour
1/2 cup whole-wheat flour
1 1/2 cups unprocessed wheat bran
1/2 cup cornmeal
1/4 to 1 teaspoon salt to taste
1 teaspoon baking soda
*2 teaspoons double-acting baking
    powder*

Scoop the sour cream into the baking pan of your bread machine, add the water and molasses, and break in the egg. If you like raisins in your brown bread, toss in a cupful of them here. Because this bread is baked on a quick cycle, whole raisins will survive the kneading process relatively intact. If your machine has an interruptible mix cycle, the raisins can be added separately instead, after all the other ingredients have been blended together. Measure in the all-purpose and whole-wheat flours, the wheat bran and cornmeal, and the salt. Scatter the baking soda and baking powder more or less evenly over these dry ingredients.

Bake on your machine's quick cycle.

Zucchini Bread

This recipe doesn't use enough zucchini to solve the surplus problem for those with zucchini in their summer gardens. But the presence of the vegetable among the ingredients ensures a moist and flavorful bread. Raisins, pecans, or walnuts can be added for extra goodness. I'd vote for the pecans.

You might note that, beyond the honey and eggs, no liquid is called for. The zucchini, being 99 percent water, supplies plenty.

> ½ cup honey
> 2 eggs
> ½ cup unsalted butter
> 1 teaspoon vanilla extract
> 1 cup zucchini, finely chopped
> 1 cup raisins, pecans, or walnuts
>   (optional)
> 2 cups unbleached all-purpose flour
> ½ teaspoon cinnamon
> ¼ to 1 teaspoon salt to taste
> ½ teaspoon baking soda
> 1 teaspoon double-acting baking
>   powder

Place the honey and eggs in your bread machine's baking pan and add the butter, cut into small chunks if it's hard, since you are using a sizable quantity, so that it will blend with the other ingredients better. Then add the vanilla extract, the chopped zucchini, and the raisins or nuts if desired. Next, add the flour, cinnamon, salt, baking soda, and baking powder, taking care to sprinkle the last two over the other ingredients rather than spooning them into one spot, so they will be distributed uniformly throughout the dough.

Use a quick bake cycle for this loaf.

Irish Currant Bread

Here's a lovely tea bread that's brimming with currants. A festive version of Irish soda bread, this loaf uses baking powder.

Now before I get a bushel of letters remonstrating that real Irish soda bread is made with baking soda alone, none of this fancy baking-powder stuff, thank you, let me say that no one is more aware of this discrepancy than I.

In point of fact, for quite some time I had a whole row of diminutive rock-hard loaves aspiring to be Irish soda bread lined up by the "brick factory," as our daughter Tanya dubbed my bread machine the week the queue began forming at the rear of the kitchen counter. They were the result of a fortnight of trying to devise an all-soda Irish soda bread recipe that would work in a bread machine. It couldn't be done.

Soda doesn't have much staying power as a leavening agent, and even the shortest cycle of a bread machine is such that by the time baking begins, the soda is no longer generating any carbon dioxide to raise the dough. If you increase the quantity of soda in a recipe to the point where it works — well, barely, anyway — in a bread machine, the loaf emerges smelling like old fish.

So, strictly speaking, the bread presented here is not a genuine Irish soda bread, simply because it is not leavened by soda. In all else, however, it is true to its heritage, right down to the tea.

The designation of this particular loaf as a tea bread derives not from the happenstance that the bread is often served with the proverbial Irish cuppa, but from the fact that the liquid used in it really is tea. Tea is acidic, and is what in the original recipe, designed for conventional baking, sent the baking soda on its bubbly way. Here, it still adds flavor and color. And the loaf, baking powder notwithstanding, is still delicious.

To continue the tradition of tending a soda bread to its proper conclusion, let the loaf cool on a rack. Then wrap it in a just-damp linen towel and let it set overnight. Slice very thin and serve with sweet butter.

1 cup tea, room temperature to tepid
1 egg
1 cup dried currants
2 cups unbleached all-purpose flour
1 cup firmly packed dark brown sugar
¼ to 1 teaspoon salt to taste
1 tablespoon double-acting baking
powder

Pour the tea into the baking pan of your bread machine, break the egg into it, and toss in the currants, making sure they're not all stuck together. Add the flour, brown sugar, salt, and baking powder.

Bake on your machine's quick cycle.

Teff Nut Bread

Teff is an ancient grain grown in the highlands of Ethiopia, where it has been used for centuries to make bread. Traditionally esteemed for its reputedly rich nutritional value and high iron content, it makes a terrific ultra-fine-grained bread. The flour is available in this country from sources listed in the back of the book.

At first, buying flour from Ethiopia seemed to me like arrogantly robbing the starving of their last means of sustenance. Then I realized that teff flour is probably one of that poverty- and war-ravaged country's few exportable items and a means of earning desperately needed foreign exchange. So, with a clearer conscience, I began experimenting. This teff nut bread recipe is a notable result.

In many parts of North Africa, nomadic peoples have been known to live for months on dates and camel's milk alone. The combination, as it so happens, is an almost perfect diet nutritionally. Camel's milk is in rather short supply in the part of Connecticut where we live, but the addition of whole cow's milk, dates, and nuts to the already nutritious teff flour results in a loaf that is truly a meal in itself.

Teff flour looks like a light-colored cocoa powder, so it's not surprising that bread made from it is very dark even when baked on a light machine setting. Don't be disappointed to see a smallish, quite compact loaf the color of a chocolate bar emerge from your pan; it will not be burned. You'll find the texture unbelievably silky for a bread. Superb spread with just sweet butter or a mild, soft cheese, delicate slices of it make an excellent selection for an old-fashioned high tea.

> 1 cup whole milk
> 1 egg
> ¼ cup unsalted butter or canola oil
> ½ cup pecans, coarsely chopped
> ½ cup dates, chopped
> 1½ cups teff flour
> ½ cup firmly packed dark brown sugar
> 1 teaspoon cinnamon (optional)
> ¼ to 1 teaspoon salt to taste
> ½ teaspoon baking soda
> 2 teaspoons double-acting baking powder

If a preliminary bread-mixing setting is available on your machine, the nutmeats and dates in this recipe can be reserved and added separately, after the initial blending of the other ingredients, to remain as chunkier bits in the finished loaf. Otherwise, place the milk and egg in the baking pan of your bread machine and add the butter, first cutting it into small chunks if it's hard so it will blend with the other ingredients better, or substitute canola oil if you prefer. Add the chopped pecans and dates next, then the flour, brown sugar, cinnamon if desired, and salt. Scatter the baking soda and baking powder evenly over the other ingredients for better blending.

Use a quick bake cycle for this bread.

Peanut Butter Bread

A peanut butter bread might seem to be overdoing things a bit. But there's a good nutritional reason for combining peanuts with the wheat of flour. Peanuts, besides being a good source of the B vitamin niacin, not to mention fiber, are an excellent protein. However, their protein is incomplete, lacking several important amino acids. Wheat and dairy products, on the other hand, provide the missing amino acids and thus complement the peanuts admirably.

Besides, if the peanut butter is already in the bread, as our ever-practical child Revell observed while putting up his school lunch one day, "all you need is the jelly."

Peanut butter is ordinarily salty enough so that no additional salt is needed for this bread. However, if what you have around the house is the unsalted variety, as is true in our home, you might want to add a dash or two of salt, though I don't.

> *1 cup milk, whole or skim*
> *1 egg*
> *⅔ cup smooth peanut butter*
> *1½ cups unbleached all-purpose flour*
> *¼ cup firmly packed dark brown sugar*
> *4 teaspoons double-acting baking powder*

Pour the milk into your baking pan, break the egg into the milk, and ladle in the peanut butter, followed by the flour, brown sugar, and baking powder, unless for your particular machine the leavening is to be placed in the pan first and covered with the rest of the dry ingredients before the liquids are added, in which case the order should be reversed.

Set your machine on quick bake for this bread.

Banana Bread

My first attempts to turn out a satisfactory banana bread using a bread machine were quite sticky endeavors. The customary recipes for this traditional bake-sale and potluck-supper standard, which produce golden, moist loaves from an ordinary oven, consistently produced from the electronic oven a loaf with a soft, gooey — in fact, soggy — spot at top center. On the other hand, the recipes to be found in any of the bread machine booklets I perused yielded coarse loaves tasting as if banana skins, rather than the fruit pulp itself, had been used for flavoring.

Looking at the baking process in a bread machine from an engineering point of view — oh, all right, from the point of view of a year's worth of mostly forgotten college physics, if the truth must be known — I decided that the kind of rich, velvety loaf characteristic of traditional banana bread required a denser, moister dough than the machine was designed to deal with. That meant either redesigning the machine or modifying one of my recipes to compensate for the persistence of a relatively cool spot at the center top of the pan during the baking process. A smaller, squatter loaf should work. It did.

The recipe given here makes a modestly sized loaf, but an exceedingly tasty one. As with any banana bread, one of the secrets of success is to have on hand bananas that are truly ripe. Their skins should be well flecked with brown. But the loaf itself takes literally only a minute or two of preparation time.

¼ cup buttermilk
1 egg
¼ cup unsalted butter or canola oil
1 teaspoon vanilla extract
½ cup mashed ripe banana
1 cup unbleached all-purpose flour
½ cup sugar
¼ to 1 teaspoon salt to taste
¼ teaspoon baking soda
2 teaspoons double-acting baking powder

Measure the buttermilk into the baking pan of your bread machine, break the egg into it, and add the butter, cutting it into chunks if it's hard so it can more easily be mixed with the other ingredients, or substitute canola oil, if you prefer. Then add the vanilla. Scoop in the mashed banana, add the flour, sugar, and salt, and scatter the baking soda and baking powder over the dry ingredients.

Bake on your machine's quick cycle.

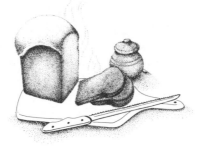

13 · Glazes: The Designer's Touch

THE QUINTESSENCE of a bread is revealed in its crust. The color and texture and aroma of that crown tell the tale of the whole loaf, and the flavor is at its fullest there.

Glazing in bread making evolved to highlight that crust; and garnishes, to announce the loaves' contents. Witness the tradition of rolled oats on oatmeal bread and, more obliquely, the poppy seeds that came to be the distinctive signature of an egg loaf. Designer bread, if you will, may be visually more important in bread machine baking, which produces loaves quite often similar in shape and size and color, than it is in traditional baking, where the dough can be shaped in quite distinctive ways.

In conventional baking, a glaze is brushed over a loaf of bread either just before it's popped into the oven to bake or just after it's pulled from the rack, still warm and mellow. In the case of the bread machine bakery, only the latter option is available. Still, most glazes work splendidly on loaves fresh from these compact electronic ovens, and they do add that visual finishing touch that somehow, even though it's not crucial, makes the bread taste even better.

Glazes are matters of personal preference. I wouldn't use a molasses glaze or put rolled oats on an egg bread. Let me amend that: I wouldn't put rolled oats on an egg bread, and I've never used a molasses glaze on it, either. But, come to think of it, a nice mahogany molasses glaze might go rather well with an egg bread. Maybe I'll give it a try.

Where the boundary between glazes and frostings lies I've never been sure. Powdered sugar mixed with water or warm milk and drizzled over a Danish ring as an underlay for extra nuts really seems to me to be a frosting, yet is considered a glaze. Then again, a Danish coffee cake, the "cake" in its name notwithstanding, is actually a very rich bread, not a cake. So maybe the dividing line between glaze and frosting has more to do with the one between bread and cake than with anything else.

Semantics aside, in today's innovative world of breads anything goes — well, almost anything. I'd still have to think about rolled oats some before I tried them on that egg bread. But experiment to see what works for you.

Egg Glaze

Here's a glaze that complements almost any loaf of bread. Small seeds sprinkled over it add a decorative visual accent.

> 1 egg
> 1 tablespoon water or milk, whole or skim
> small seeds for garnish — poppy, caraway,
>   sesame — or, for Scandinavian coffee
>   breads, pearl sugar

Break the egg into a bowl and whip it with the water or milk. As soon as you've taken your bread from the bread machine, close the lid of the machine to keep the oven warm. While the bread is still in its pan and hot, paint the top of the loaf with the glazing mixture, using a pastry brush. If the bread is a dense one that looks as if it might need a bit of shaking to loosen from the pan, knock it out first, to make sure it won't give you any trouble later, after it's been glazed. Then slip it right back into the pan before brushing it with the egg wash.

Sprinkle small seeds such as poppy seeds, caraway seeds, or sesame seeds liberally over the glaze. For Scandinavian coffee breads, use pearl sugar.

Pop the pan back into the still-warm bread machine for two or three minutes and let the residual heat from your electronic oven bake the glaze to a nice gloss.

Salt Wash

Used primarily on a crusty white bread, and normally brushed onto a loaf before baking, a simple salt wash adds a little extra savor even when applied to a finished loaf.

¹⁄₄ cup hot water
1 teaspoon salt

Dissolve the salt in the water and brush this briny wash over your bread as it comes hot from the oven. Then put the loaf back into the warm bread machine for a few minutes to dry the glaze.

Molasses Glaze

Molasses adds a dark sheen to hearty ryes, pumpernickels, and raisin breads. Use it with restraint, however, lest it remain too sticky.

> *1 tablespoon unsulphured molasses*
> *1 tablespoon hot water*
> *dehydrated onion flakes or small seeds*
> *   for garnish (optional)*

Stir the molasses and water together briskly and spread liberally over the top of your bread with a soft brush as soon as the loaf is removed from your electronic oven. In the case of a solid loaf such as a country rye or pumpernickel, knock the loaf out of its pan first to ensure that it won't give you trouble later, then return it to the container before applying the glaze.

Sprinkle dehydrated onion flakes or some other attractive garnish such as black sesame seeds or flaxseed over the molasses if you'd like. Then return the loaf to the still-warm bread machine briefly to firm the gloss on.

Oil Wash

Oil washes are used predominantly on herb and savory breads to give them a soft luster. Fresh, bright herbs, finely minced and sprinkled over them, add a finishing sparkle to most loaves in either category.

1 egg
1½ to 2 teaspoons olive oil
fresh herbs, chopped fine (optional)

Break the egg into a small bowl and whip till frothy. Add slowly, beating lightly between additions, enough olive oil to make a smooth blend. Brush this mix over your bread while it's still hot from the oven and, if desired, sprinkle herbs over it to garnish the loaf. Return the bread, in its pan, to the hot bread machine briefly to set the glaze.

Confectioners' Sugar Glaze

More than an everyday glaze, less than a frosting, a powdered sugar gloss adds a delicate confectionery touch to a loaf of bread. Sweet glazes are usually reserved for coffee breads and cakes, but they occasionally grace a plain milk bread intended for a festive brunch.

1 cup confectioners' sugar
2 to 3 tablespoons water or warm milk,
    whole or skim

Sift the powdered sugar into a small bowl and add the liquid a few drops at a time, beating until smooth and dribbly. Drizzle over warm bread just out of its baking pan. Spiral and crisscross patterns are becoming.

Flavored Sugar Glazes

A sugar glaze is capable of almost infinite variation. Substitute a few drops of vanilla or almond extract for part of the milk or water in the preceding basic confectioners' sugar glaze, or dispense with the suggested liquids altogether and use coffee or rum or brandy instead if one of those flavorings would suit the bread and your taste. Replace a couple of spoonfuls of the powdered sugar with cocoa if appropriate, or add a dash of cinnamon or nutmeg or some other spice if it would bring out the flavor of the loaf. Just don't let your glaze overpower the bread it's meant to merely accent.

A Sugar Dusting

A dusting of powdered sugar is technically not, by itself, a glaze. But if you keep a shaker can of confectioners' sugar within easy reach of your bread machine, it takes only a second to turn a scrumptious almond loaf or a delectable banana bread into a visual delight as well. A feathery dusting of pure white sugar, maybe even shaken through a lace doily for an intricate pattern against the background of a golden crust, has almost irresistible appeal.

14 · After the Loaf

W ITHIN A FEW WEEKS of acquiring a bread machine, many people find that loading it up and setting it in action have become as much a part of the daily routine as loading up the Brewmaster for the morning's coffee is. An inevitable by-product of this pleasant ritual is leftover bread — not all that much of it, mind you, because the hot-from-the-electronic-oven loaves are too tempting to pass up, but with fresh bread always available, one hates to settle for day-old.

We have chickens. They're one answer to the leftovers problem. They get the old bread scraps and we recycle the newly laid eggs in new bread.

A solution to the stale-bread conundrum easier for most people to implement is recycling the bread itself. One form of such reuse popular in our family is bread pudding. Bread pudding, I might add, isn't simply bread pudding anymore once your pantry is stocked with the variety of loaves a bread machine makes probable.

Consider the matter of cardamom bread, for instance. It makes such a superlative bread pudding that even when we use regular bread for the pudding, we now add a little cardamom for flavoring.

For French toast, it's well worth baking a whole extra loaf of bread just for that favorite of the kids, so I really shouldn't include it here as an answer to the leftovers quandary. Let me confine myself to suggesting that if you do make French toast from your homemade bread, and if you slice the loaf into inch-thick slabs and let them stale for half a day or so before sinking them into their coating batter, you'll have on your breakfast or supper plates a delicacy fit for a king — or at least a *fattiga riddare,* or poor knight, as the dish is known in Sweden.

There are always stuffings, of course, and dumplings, and other entremets calling for bread, leftover or otherwise. You can always dice up extra loaves and toss the cubes in the freezer to await a Thanksgiving bird needing dressing or some entrée to which dumplings would be a perfect accompaniment. But these are probably occasional recyclings at best.

Melba toast, or twice-baked bread, is a practical end for your loaves. It's a noble foil for pâtés, and it suits dips well, making a flavorsome low-salt substitute for chips. Cut some firm day-old bread into slices about a quarter of an inch thick. Don't limit yourself to white. Experiment. Place the slices on an ungreased cookie sheet and bake them in an oven preheated to 325 degrees F. until they are crisp and golden. They're best served fresh — if you'll pardon my use of that term in connection with stale bread — hot from the oven.

Take the same bread and slice it a little thicker, maybe in pieces a half to three-quarters of an inch across, then cross-cut these slices into cubes. Sauté them in a mix of half butter and half olive oil until they are crisp and just one step past golden brown. Drain them on paper towels, and you have croutons, not the cardboard kind found in salad bars, but real ones, crunchy islands of flavor with which to garnish green pea and other creamy soups.

Or, while the croutons are sautéing, toss in some freshly pressed garlic. Then, at the last minute, as you pull the pan from the fire, sprinkle the cubes with Parmesan cheese, a little extra melted butter, and some finely minced parsley. These croutons are matchless for adding crunch and contrast to a salad. Try making them from pumpernickel or rye bread.

Even bread crumbs taste fresher and better when they're home-made. If you choose this means of disposing of your bakery leftovers, remember that the crust is the most flavorful part of a loaf. Bread heels make the best crumbs of all.

To toast the crumbs, simply dice some stale bread into quarter-inch squares, place them on an ungreased cookie sheet, and oven-dry them at 300 degrees F. for thirty to forty-five minutes. Let them cool, then grind them to the fineness desired, in small batches, in your blender or food processor. Stored in an airtight container, they will keep for a month or more on your pantry shelf.

Besides providing excellent crumbs, bread crusts make wonderful dog bones, of all things. My children have developed that all-American habit of slicing off the heel, or cornerhouse, as it's referred to in Germany, of a loaf and helping themselves to the second slice in. How on earth this custom evolved in our family I don't know, since the heel, well slathered with butter, is my favorite part of the bread. Nevertheless, there it is, and one time when we were accumulating heels, which aren't all that great for bread pudding, and had more than enough bread crumbs on hand, I gave a couple to our dogs, Crisscross and Zechy. They loved the rye.

Ever since, whenever there's a surfeit of leftover bread, I cut slices of the dark, heavy loaves into oblong thirds and let them air-dry on a rack for a couple of days, by this simple feat transforming them into dog bones. I'll bet when the Japanese invented the bread machine, they had no idea how happy our dogs were going to be.

Sources for Baking Ingredients

 MORE AND MORE GROCERY STORES, even large supermarkets, now carry specialty flours and other exotic baking ingredients not found on their shelves a mere few years ago, and what isn't located there can often be procured from one or another of the health-food and alternative-lifestyle shops proliferating in many areas of the country. Still, a few of the rarer flours may not be found even there, and some of us live far from such emporiums. Here mail order often comes to the rescue, and the catalogs and other literature available from the mail-order houses frequently make inspirational reading. The following are sources I have found helpful in my bread-baking ventures.

Birkett Mills
P.O. Box 440
Penn Yan, NY 14527
Tel. (315) 536-3311

FREE PRICE LIST
NO CREDIT CARDS ACCEPTED

This mill specializes in buckwheat products, carrying flour, stone-ground groats, even seeds for sprouting.

Brewster River Mills
Mill Street
Jeffersonville, VT 05464
Tel. (802) 644-2287

FREE BROCHURE

ACCEPTS MASTERCARD AND VISA CREDIT CARDS

Organic flours and meals are available from this supplier.

Jaffe Bros., Inc.
P.O. Box 636
Valley Center, CA 92082
Tel. (619) 749-1133

FREE CATALOG

ACCEPTS MASTERCARD AND VISA CREDIT CARDS

This firm features a large selection of organic grains, flours, and meals.

Kenyon Corn Meal Co.
Usquepaugh
West Kingston, RI 02892
Tel. (401) 783-4054

FREE PRICE LIST

ACCEPTS MASTERCARD AND VISA CREDIT CARDS

Various flours and mixes are available through this supplier.

King Arthur Flour
RR 2, Box 56
Norwich, VT 05055
Tel. (800) 827-6836

FREE CATALOG

ACCEPTS MASTERCARD AND VISA CREDIT CARDS

This firm carries all the basic flours along with some unusual ones such as teff.

G. B. Ratto & Co.
821 Washington Street
Oakland, CA 94607
Tel. (800) 325-3483

FREE CATALOG

ACCEPTS MASTERCARD AND VISA CREDIT CARDS

This firm carries a wide variety of flours and meals, including chestnut and garbanzo, as well as sourdough starter.

Walnut Acres
Penns Creek, PA 17862
Tel. (800) 433-3998

FREE CATALOG

ACCEPTS MASTERCARD AND VISA CREDIT CARDS

This company carries flours from millet to teff as well as sourdough starter.

Index